D1362182

Tradition » Passion » Perfection

Marilisa Racco was born into a fashion family and knew her Versace from her Valentino before she could talk. Based in Toronto, Canada, she has written for *ELLE Canada, Sportswear International, BlackBook,* and *FLARE* and *Style* magazines, and is a beauty columnist for *The Globe and Mail.* Racco also writes about the fashion industry on her blog, The Chic Storm.

Princeton Architectural Press
37 East Seventh Street
New York, NY 10003
Visit our website at www.papress.com

Conceived and produced by
Elwin Street Productions
3 Percy Street
London W1T 1DE
www.elwinstreet.com

Illustrations: Tonwen Jones
Photo credits: Sussie Ahlberg: pp. 37, 61, 97;
Getty: pp. 105, 119; Don Spiro: p. 91; Josh Verleun: p. 45;
Richard Warren: p. 27

Library of Congress Cataloging-in-Publication Data
Racco, Marilisa.
Lingerie / Marilisa Racco. — First edition.
pages cm — (Instant expert: tradition, passion,
perfection)
Includes bibliographical references and index.
ISBN 978-1-61689-250-0 (alk. paper)
1. Lingerie. I. Title.
TT670.R33 2014
646.4'204—dc23
2013028079

Why be an expert about lingerie?

It might sit in the same drawer with your daily cottons and utilitarian spandex, but lingerie is not merely a matter of function. As in the grand tradition of couture, lingerie depends on art and meticulousness to create a product of unprecedented quality and luxury.

There's a lot to be said for feeling comfortable and confident in your clothes and even more to be said for feeling the same way under your clothes. Over the centuries, lingerie has run the gamut from the purely functional loincloths and fabric swathes of the Greeks and Romans to the elaborate petticoats and downright torturous corsets of the Victorians. When the brassiere finally made its appearance at the dawn of the Jazz Age, it liberated women in both dress and attitude and signaled a dramatic shift in societal standards and gender politics.

By the time the mid-twentieth century gave birth to an anti-conformist call to burn the bra, and then did a swift about-face with decidedly risqué thongs and push-up bras marketed as daily wear, it was clear that lingerie had as much to do with the fabric of history as satin and lace.

Derived from the French word *linge*, which means washables, lingerie encompasses everything that was worn by women beneath their clothes to propagate modesty, hygiene, and the reproductive female form. But despite its early utilitarian purpose, luxury laces, silks, and trims became the hallmark of an exclusive garment that belonged to an artistic heritage and an elevated echelon of society.

The story behind luxury lingerie does not lie in duchesses and debutantes, but artisans and engineers—the people behind great construction and eye-popping design. Much like an impressive work of architecture, fine lingerie depends on mathematically precise measurement as well as a beautiful façade. In lingerie, it truly is what's inside that counts.

The true lingerie lover makes it her mission to seek out the best-fitting bra, one that lifts and separates, hugs and caresses, and makes her expensive blouse look even more exclusive. She recognizes lingerie's inherent ability to make her move with more grace, stand with more authority, and seduce with greater aplomb. And for their part, the lingerie brands respond in kind with a product that addresses her every need, from boudoir to boardroom, to please on all levels and which defies the odds of, say, taking years off your décolletage and pounds off your hips. But most of all, they adhere to a tradition of quality and luxury and offer something for everyone. Democracy at its finest.

When it comes to lingerie, snobbery is not price-tag specific. It hinges on finding the best fit for your figure and the best silhouette for your proportions. When you consider that a good bra is composed of twenty-five different parts that are painstakingly cut, measured and sewn, and that being even one-eighth of an inch off in construction means the difference between an exceptional fit and a garment that feels like a medieval torture device, it makes fine lingerie as important to a woman's wardrobe as the little black dress. Too much cleavage with a low-cut blouse or a sagging bust in a body-conscious top can spell disaster for the most fashion-conscious woman. It means the difference between a push-up or a balconette, a full or a demi-cup—all of which reside in the world of luxury lingerie.

But it isn't just practicality—lingerie also links to more esoteric notions, ones of feeling and attitude. The act of slipping into a lace bra or satin panties has the unique ability to transform a mundane task into a quietly luxurious daily experience. It's a purely personal extravagance that can make you move and act differently, with more confidence and grace. That's why it is worth taking a little time to understand and recognize the hallmarks of beautifully made lingerie.

» Fundamentals

Lingerie or underwear?

When you think of underwear, oftentimes visions of white high-rise briefs come to mind—the proverbial "granny pant," if you will. While this can have its place in your lingerie drawer (if it must), it is hardly the kind of undergarment you'll reach for when prepping for a big night or before slipping into your favorite low-rise jeans.

However, there's a misconception that "lingerie" should be relegated to those aforementioned big nights, when in fact it is as practical on a daily basis as "granny pants." With superior construction in mind and use of natural, breathable, as well as beautiful fabrics, fine lingerie beats Lycra thongs and molded bras in the day-to-day category. But what about the high cost of lingerie? If you don't think twice about spending thousands on a handbag and list craftsmanship and quality of construction among the reasons to justify it, then think the same way about lingerie, but add in its ability to make you look larger or smaller chested, with thinner thighs or a more whittled waist. A handbag cannot do that!

Price and quality

What's even more disconcerting is that the mass-market brands, for what they offer, are in fact over-priced. While they draw in customers with flashy ad campaigns and extravagant runway presentations, luxury lingerie companies focus their budgets on creating quality garments and have a smaller advertising presence. Whose undergarments would you rather buy: a supermodel's or the ones that will make you look thinner and feel better?

Matching lingerie sets

It's hard to tell if the match mentality is one that derives from age or culture. With regard to ready-to-wear, matching can be seen as belonging to a bygone era when women coordinated their shoes with their handbags and which today is relegated to ladies of a certain generation. However, when talking about lingerie, the same woman who might scoff at matching her Birkin to her ballerinas most likely is adamant about ensuring her bra and panties are a perfect set.

Mother of invention

By the first decade of the twentieth century, women's fashions started to shed their voluminous silhouette in favor of a more streamlined look, making corsets bulky and unsightly. When Mary Phelps Jacob, a New York socialite, slipped into a chiffon gown for an event one night she shuddered at the sight of the whalebone in her corset poking out from her plunging neckline. So with the help of her maid, Jacob fashioned a rudimentary bra out of silk handkerchiefs and some pink ribbon. On November 3, 1914, she was awarded a patent for the "Backless Brassiere."

Some experts argue this comes down to the classic geographic divide. That Europeans, who are the original lingerie connoisseurs, would never dream of wearing a mismatched set, while Americans, who are more pragmatic in their way of dressing, are the purveyors of the mix-and-match and view the functional black bra as the perfect complement to even the laciest pink thong.

Mix and match

But what it really boils down to is preference. Yes, it's true that the lingerie aficionado buys a matching set with an extra matching panty (because the panties will be washed more frequently and will submit to more wear-and-tear), but even the most exclusive lingerie brands are now offering mix-and-match sets. There is always a common thread that binds a theme—maybe it's a black bra with white polka dots that has a corresponding white panty with black polka dots, or a red bra with a floral ribbon that matches to a blue panty with the same ribbon detail—but black-with-black and lace-with-lace is no longer the hard-and-fast rule to buying lingerie.

Bear in mind that a red lace bustier does not make a companion of white cotton briefs, but know that the choice is always yours. If you can artfully clash your Birkin with your ballerinas, then your lingerie can be equally avant-garde and always chic.

» How to evaluate a good bra

013

A quality brassiere will feel and fit as well as it looks. The moment you slip it on you will be able to tell if it isn't a quality garment. If it gapes in the cup area, if the band rides up too high in the back, if the straps slip off your shoulders or if you feel the underwire digging into your skin, don't buy it! Run your fingers along the seams of the underwire and the closure. If it pricks or itches, it's not a quality bra.

Then there is the issue of fabric. Most high-end European lingerie brands work directly with lace manufacturers throughout the continent or have their own lace designers in-house, like Lise Charmel. A fine lace should never be rough or itchy, and while it's not as sturdy as, say, a Lycra-satin blend, it should still offer some elasticity, hold you up, and shape your bust. When testing a fabric's elasticity, it should easily bounce back when you pull at it, without showing the indent of your fingers in the fabric.

Bra styles

Thanks to international influence and the ever-revolving door of trends, a bra is no longer just a bra. The bevy of lingerie styles on offer is undoubtedly thrilling, but it can also be challenging to keep the terminology straight. If you are having a hard time telling your balconette from your bandeau, this guide will help you navigate the sea of styles.

Balconette A quarter-cup style with minimal coverage that is cut horizontally across the breast; offers lift and enhances cleavage.

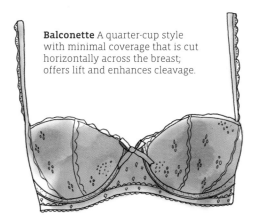

Bandeau A swathe of fabric that wraps all around the torso and can come with or without padding; often trimmed with silicone to prevent slipping.

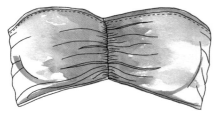

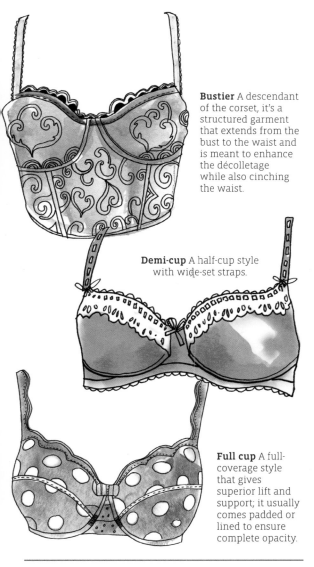

Bustier A descendant of the corset, it's a structured garment that extends from the bust to the waist and is meant to enhance the décolletage while also cinching the waist.

Demi-cup A half-cup style with wide-set straps.

Full cup A full-coverage style that gives superior lift and support; it usually comes padded or lined to ensure complete opacity.

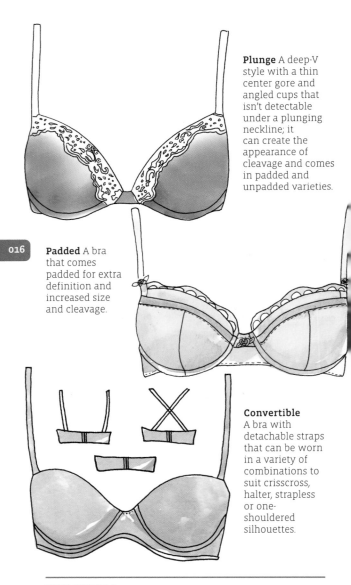

Plunge A deep-V style with a thin center gore and angled cups that isn't detectable under a plunging neckline; it can create the appearance of cleavage and comes in padded and unpadded varieties.

Padded A bra that comes padded for extra definition and increased size and cleavage.

Convertible A bra with detachable straps that can be worn in a variety of combinations to suit crisscross, halter, strapless or one-shouldered silhouettes.

Push-up A bra with angled cups, underwire and graduated padding that is thicker under the bust but tapers off toward the top; it pushes the breasts together and up, creating the illusion of a larger size as well as cleavage.

Shelf Traditionally, this is a bra that has an underwire with little or no cup coverage, but in modern parlance this is also used to describe built-in support in clothing or swimwear.

Triangle A triangular neckline created by triangle-shaped cups with thin straps; it usually comes with no underwire and is suited to petite shapes.

Brief styles

Bikini A style that offers full coverage in the back with thin straps at the sides; ranges from high- to low-cut.

Brief A full-coverage style with a medium-rise.

Thong A bikini-style front with fabric of varying thickness that runs across the hips and down the back, fully exposing the buttocks.

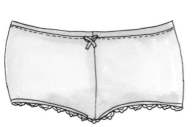

Boyshort A medium- to low-cut style that gives full coverage across the hips and buttocks and extends to just above the thigh.

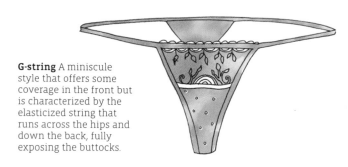

G-string A miniscule style that offers some coverage in the front but is characterized by the elasticized string that runs across the hips and down the back, fully exposing the buttocks.

Front

Brazilian A shrunken version of any type of underpants (brief, boyshort, bikini); coverage ranges from exposing half the buttock to G-string style; it's usually low cut and sexy.

Back

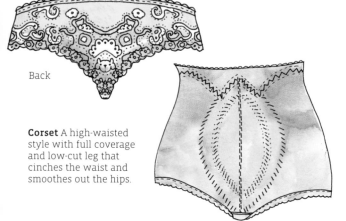

Corset A high-waisted style with full coverage and low-cut leg that cinches the waist and smoothes out the hips.

Lingerie drawer essentials

With so many different styles of bras and briefs on the market, it can be difficult to determine necessity versus frivolity. Here is a list of essentials to help you on your way:

Bras

»	**An all-purpose bra with full support and coverage**
»	**A strapless bra**
»	**A convertible bra**
»	**A bustier bra**

Briefs

»	**A laser-cut brief to eliminate the appearance of lines**
»	**A laser-cut thong**
»	**A low-rise brief**
»	**A high-rise brief**
»	**A control-top brief**

Extras

»	**A fancy camisole that can double as a blouse**
»	**A fancy bodysuit that can be worn under a suit jacket**
»	**A control-top bodysuit that smoothes out the appearance of bulges**
»	**Control-top tights**
»	**A shapewear garment covering from below the bust to mid-thigh**

When deciding what colors to invest in, black, nude, and ivory are always smart choices, but also consider pastels in lieu of ivory and muted shades of pink, lavender, and yellow as alternatives to nude.

Words from the wise

Vasilia Panagakos Owner of luxury lingerie boutique Avec Plaisir, Toronto, Canada

» Debunking bra myths

There are several common bra myths that are sure to land you in an uncomfortable and unflattering bra. First up is the idea that a bra should be fastened on the loosest hook. This isn't a concern with a quality bra—the three hooks are there for your comfort.

Another common myth is that the wider the bra strap, the more supportive it will be. In fact, the support comes from all aspects—fabric, accuracy of construction, and pattern—which means good support is not contingent on straps. A well-constructed bra should still hold you up even if you slip off the straps. Likewise, strapless bras are not about a tighter fit. If the cup size of a strapless bra isn't correct, it will still slip. This has nothing to do with tightness and everything to do with fit. Also misleading is the idea that more cleavage means more support. Unless your bra pushes your bust up, you are not getting the right amount of support.

Choosing the right lingerie for your shape

Lingerie is all about aesthetics—your aesthetic, that is. Be it a delicate lace demi-cup with Swarovski embellishment or a white cotton triangle bra, the bottom line is that it has to make you look and feel good. Determining which item is best suited to your body type is a tricky task that relies as much on want as it does on need. You may, for example, want to wear the delicate lace demi-cup, but your bust may demand something more substantial.

Shape and aims

The first thing you need to decide is what you are trying to achieve with your lingerie: Do you want to minimize what you have or enhance it? Is office appropriateness your biggest concern or are you looking to be a little more risqué? You may think you've got all these concerns covered with your wardrobe, but without the proper undergarments you might as well wear the same outfit every day because the end result will not match up to your desired image.

Enhancing

If you're small-breasted and wish to enhance your figure, invest in a good push-up bra. By padding the underside of the breast, a push-up bra lifts and squeezes together the bust to quite literally push it up while also creating cleavage. If, however, you wish to give only the illusion of a larger bust without creating cleavage, try a padded bra with foam cups. This will make your bust appear larger in size but won't expose cleavage if you're wearing a low-cut or V-neck top.

Support

A full-cup bra is best for large-breasted women who want good support but don't want to amp up their cleavage. The underwire, wide straps, and high back in this style will lift and separate the breasts, while the full coverage will limit cleavage exposure. If you have a generous bust and want to celebrate it, opt for an unpadded demi-cup. Once again the underwire, parallel back strap, and wide-set shoulder straps will provide good support, while the low-cut silhouette of this bra will allow you to show some décolletage without being too risqué.

Briefs

Briefs are a little more *à ton goût*, although certain circumstances call for particular briefs. To avoid panty lines, opt for a thong or G-string style, although many boyshorts also do away with visible lines, thanks to a low-cut leg that hits below the buttocks. For a full-coverage pant that offers support in the tummy area, try a corset pant. This style extends above the navel and has a low-cut leg that serves to cinch the waist while also shaping the hips. The bikini and brief styles both offer full coverage in the back, although the bikini has slimmer sides and is lower in cut, making it easier to wear under low-rise pants and skirts.

Bra accessories and enhancements

The world of luxury can denote a steadfast adherence to tradition that sometimes results in the message that more modern concerns are déclassé. However, when it comes to lingerie, the modern woman wants to revel as much in the luxury and tradition of its craft as she wants to look sexy and naturally endowed while wearing it. Thankfully, today the two considerations can coexist with the wide array of accessories and enhancements currently available.

Bra inserts

There is a bevy of natural-looking bra inserts on the market that work to enhance or decrease the appearance of the bust, as well as solve issues such as unevenness. To create more cleavage, slip an insert under the breast to push it upwards. If, however, you wish to decrease your bust, opt for an insert that sits on top and flattens the breast, thus minimizing a deep cleavage. Silicone inserts work well for all sizes, especially larger busts, as they mold well to a voluptuous shape, while smaller-breasted women can also choose from gel, foam, and water inserts, which are particularly effective in pushing up the bust and giving a natural-looking and -feeling lift. Foam inserts are best for swimwear as they are waterproof and won't float to the surface.

Inserts can be slipped into a designated pocket in a bra or applied directly to the breast. But if you're using an insert without a bra, you'll need a good adhesive to make sure everything stays in its place. Double-sided tape has long been the best-kept secret of celebrity stylists, but it has now also permeated the lingerie market and comes in pre-cut curved strips as well as traditional tape format. Most are either clear or nude in color so that they remain virtually undetectable.

Additional coverage

If nipple coverage is what you seek, the options are quite varied and range from adhesive stickers (or pasties, as they are colloquially known), to rounded foam cups that adhere directly to the nipple and which can be worn with or without a bra.

The bullet bra

When Christian Dior unveiled his New Look in 1947, war-weary women were ready to shed the austere utilitarianism that had ruled their wardrobes. With this new silhouette came a focus on shaping the bust to conform to womanly standards.

Enter the bullet bra. A pre-formed, conically shaped bra, it was often made of satin and nylon and used reinforced stitching to ensure exceptional lift and support. So ubiquitous and attention-grabbing was this silhouette that it gave birth to a new class of Hollywood starlets, such as Rita Hayworth and Jane Russell, dubbed Sweater Girls.

Lingerie suppliers and services

Much like the world of ready-to-wear underwear, lingerie runs the gamut from off-the-rack to made-to-measure; good lingerie can be found just as easily in a boutique as it can by visiting a bespoke designer. Specialist brands can be found around the world, often in their own branded stores, while smaller boutique labels are carried in department stores and speciality lingerie shops. It's not unusual for ready-to-wear designers to branch out into the lingerie market and sell their offerings both in conjunction with their apparel and in speciality lingerie stores. Most high-end boutiques and department stores carry a variety of labels from around the world, and while the exclusive corsetiere or designer is a little more obscure, a few of the luxury lingerie houses offer their own in-house bespoke service.

In the case of bespoke lingerie, you will be asked to make an appointment for an initial consultation and then will need to make at least one or two subsequent appointments to try on the garment in its various stages of construction.

Many lingerie outposts will also have a seamstress on hand to do any relevant alterations and can advise you on the proper care of a fine garment as well as refer you to speciality dry cleaners.

Words from the wise

Gail Epstein Cofounder, president, and creative director, Hanky Panky Ltd, New York, NY

≫ Panty fit tips

The only thing worse than a bad hair day is a bad panty day. But you needn't experience one again if you take the time to thoroughly consider your next purchase. Here are some tips for finding the perfect fit:

Try them on. Sit down, stand up, touch your toes, and generally move around to see if they stay put.

Panties should have shape in strategic areas — women are not shaped like paper dolls! Panties should also have enough shape to fit correctly and stay in place.

Avoid heavy, stiff elastics. Panty legs should be trimmed with soft, lightweight elastic or lace, otherwise you risk the dreaded VPL (Visible Panty Lines).

Price matters. Better lingerie companies spend more time developing and fitting new styles. And when in doubt, read reviews of underwear by women with your body type.

Taking measurements

Approximately 80 percent of women wear the wrong bra size, most often falling prey to the classic blunder of overestimating their band size while underestimating their cup size. The result is not only uncomfortable and unflattering, but also potentially harmful as an ill-fitting bra can lead to back pain, shoulder discomfort, and even breast-tissue damage. While it is preferable to have someone take your measurements, you can do it yourself by following these steps:

1 Put on your best-fitting bra, the one that gives you the most ideal breast shape, but not a padded or push-up style (even if it's not the right size, at least you will know where you want your breasts to sit). Stand tall but relaxed.

2 Taking a soft measuring tape, wrap the tape snugly around your rib cage, right underneath your breasts; take a breath, exhale, and note the measurement in inches, rounding up to the nearest whole number. If your measurement is even-numbered, add 4 inches to it; if it's odd-numbered, add 5 inches. For example, if your measurement is 29.5 inches, round up to 30 and add 4 inches for a measurement of 34. This is your band size.

3 Then, take the measuring tape and wrap it around the fullest part of your bust (this is usually right across the nipples), and once again round the measurement in inches up to the nearest whole number. For

example, if the measurement is 35.5 inches, round it up to 36.

4 At this point you know that your band size is 34. To calculate your cup size, subtract the cup size measurement from the band size—in this case, 36 minus 34. For every inch in difference, add a cup size, starting from an A cup. Thus, a two-inch difference means adding two cups for a final measurement of 34B.

Some women wear the wrong bra size just because they are used to buying a specific size, and they don't notice that it no longer fits very well—even small variations in your weight can have an effect on your bra size, so you should measure yourself every now and then and don't assume that just because you've always worn a 34C, that's still your size.

International size guide

Surprisingly, there is no uniform system to lingerie sizing. Most countries have their own scale, which makes it tricky to determine what your bra and brief sizes are in France versus Italy versus the United States. While most luxury brands will print a small conversion chart on the garment's label, it helps to have a basic idea of the different sizing before stepping into a lingerie boutique (see page 30).

International bra sizes

U.S.	U.K.	France	Europe	Italy
32A	32B	85B	70B	1B
32B	32C	85C	70C	1C
32C	32D	85D	70D	1D
32D	32DD	85E	70E	1E
34A	34B	90B	75B	2B
34B	34C	90C	75C	2C
34C	34D	90D	75D	2D
34D	34DD	90E	75E	2E
36A	36B	95B	80B	3B
36B	36C	95C	80C	3C
36C	36D	95D	80D	3D
36D	36DD	95E	80E	3E

International brief sizes

U.S.	U.K.	France	Europe	Italy
XS	XS (8)	38 (1)	34	2
S	S (10)	40 (2)	36	3
M	M (12)	42 (3)	38	4
L	L (14)	44 (4)	40	5
XL	XL (16)	46 (5)	42	6

» Lingerie sets

Luxury lingerie

Perhaps Dorothy Parker isn't single-handedly responsible for putting the corset to pasture in the early twentieth century when she famously stated, "brevity is the soul of lingerie," but it was a sure sign that the commonly held views on women's fashion and their role in seduction were shifting. And not a moment too soon, as those winds of change ushered in the beauty, innovation, and art that distinguish modern lingerie designs. Suddenly, the world of lingerie evolved to consider what women wanted and how they felt, and not just what fashion dictated or what men desired.

Today's world-class lingerie brands are as responsible for perpetuating passion as they are for liberating women from the shackles of tradition and stringency. Where would women be today without elasticized bra straps, underwire support, or Lycra bodysuits? By mixing artisan techniques with millennial innovations, today's luxury lingerie stands as a symbol of the modern woman—tender and tough, beautiful and brainy.

Whether you are looking for designer or specialist brands, plus-size or bespoke, there are plenty of ateliers that create luxury lingerie; the following is a selection of the very best of those. The addresses provided are for each brand's flagship store; for those brands that do not have stores, website details have been included instead.

Specialist brands

Agent Provocateur

6 Broadwick Avenue, London, W1F 8HL

Tel: +44 (0)207 439 0229,
www.agentprovocateur.com

 Sensual and irreverent, the brand Agent Provocateur was founded in 1994 by Joe Corre and Serena Rees. Since then, it has grown to include nightwear, outerwear, beauty, hosiery, accessories, and two award-winning fragrances, all of which uphold AP's standards of luxury and exclusivity.

The brand's lingerie offerings are marked by a subtle sensuousness as seen in exquisite laces layered over fine silk, cutout satin styles, ribbon accents, and pleated details. Garters, corsets, and basques feature prominently in the collection, lending it an air of vintage seduction. AP also offers an extensive bridal collection, as well as sexy maternity styles.

With creativity and innovation at the core of its advertising strategy, the brand is also known for its groundbreaking campaigns, which have starred the likes of Kylie Minogue and Kate Moss.

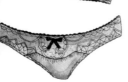

« Lingerie and suspender set from the AP Classics collection

Cosabella

760 Ocean Drive #7, Miami Beach, FL 33139

Tel: (305) 534 4731, www.cosabella.com

Taking its name from the Italian for "beautiful thing," Cosabella straddles the fine line between American design and European craftsmanship. Husband-and-wife duo Ugo and Valeria Campello founded the company in 1983 and met quasi-instant success with their signature bodysuit. Today, the company's offerings, which continue to be designed in Florida and manufactured in Italy, have grown to include other collections, such as loungewear, swimwear, beachwear, hosiery, and shapewear.

Color is at the core of Cosabella's everyday luxury philosophy and is symbolized most by the company's iconic mesh Soiré collection, which is offered in more than forty-five hues and whose thong style is the company's top-selling item. Not a brand known to rest on its laurels, Cosabella has forged ahead in the technology field with its Never Say Never collection of a colorful seamless thong in stretch lace, a corresponding push-up bra, soft bra, hot pants, chemise, and camisole.

The company proved its commitment to the environment in 2008 with the launch of the Eden and Bamboo lines made from a soft bamboo/micromodal blend, then followed it up the next year with the organic cotton Devon collection.

Eres

2 rue Tronchet, 75008, Paris

Tel: +33 (0)1 47 42 28 82, www.eresparis.com

Unlike most other high-end lingerie brands, Eres first appeared as a swimwear label and didn't branch out into the world of luxury undergarments until the late 1990s. It is likely thanks to these origins in swimwear that Eres stands out as a brand that uses fabrics as much for their luxurious look and feel as their outstanding performance.

Jersey crepe, stretch silk/cashmere, and Puy lace are the hallmarks of a brand that upholds luxury in its fabrication despite an architectural, almost Spartan aesthetic, devoid of frills and frippery. The brand pays close attention to technique and employs chain stitching and flat assembly to allow support and comfort of movement. Eres offers a full range of bra and panty styles, including swimwear and loungewear.

035

La Perla

Via Montenapoleone 1, Milan, 20121

Tel: +39 (0)2 76 00 04 60, www.laperla.com

EXPERT *Essential* It's no wonder La Perla is synonymous with luxury when you consider that founder Ada Masotti was inspired by velvet-lined jewelry cases when she named her brand in 1954. Purchases made in her boutique in Bologna at the time were packaged in red velvet-lined boxes before being transported to customers. A corsetiere by trade, Masotti distinguished her creations with techniques exclusive to fine artisans,

» Soutache and frastaglio

Soutache (pictured) is a decorative trim used to conceal a seam and a technique indicative of a luxury product. Made primarily of a high-quality material, soutache consists of flat, narrow loops similar to a ribbon that are attached by hand on fabric in an intricate pattern. It can be woven of a metallic thread, silk, or a silk-wool blend, although in today's mass-produced clothes, it more commonly uses rayon. In luxury lingerie and swimwear, soutache represents one of the most sophisticated types of workmanship.

Frastaglio is an antique type of Florentine workmanship. A technique that dates back to the eighteenth century, frastaglio is characterized by flat-stitched embroidery that is hand-trimmed to cord yarn on a veil of tulle, which is then hand-stitched to silk or another fabric. The effect obtained is a refined inlay motif that seems to climb up the fabric. It is primarily used in silk corsetry and nightwear, and is still carried out today entirely by hand.

such as soutache and frastaglio, both of which are still used in La Perla's creations today.

By the 1980s, La Perla had blossomed into a world-renowned lingerie company that included a sister line, Malizia by La Perla, which was geared to a younger and more whimsical customer, as well as the sophisticated AnnaClub line of swimwear. In 2008, the brand launched La Perla Limited Edition, an exclusive collection of "jewelry-lingerie" that uses precious stones and fine metal details, such as 14-karat gold fibers.

Although rooted in the world of lingerie, La Perla also has a ready-to-wear fashion line and recently joined forces with Jean Paul Gaultier to create Collection Créateur, a capsule collection of exclusive pieces including a corset, bustier, and a bodysuit with pointed cups reminiscent of the creations he designed for Madonna's 1990 Blond Ambition tour.

« Greta balconette and short, by La Perla

Lise Charmel

www.lisecharmel.com

Based in Lyon, France's silk capital, Lise Charmel was founded in the 1950s with notions of luxury and creativity at its core. The company comprises more than one thousand employees who collectively produce four collections per year—two more than most other lingerie houses. The result is a brand that stands as much for tradition and craftsmanship as it does for new technologies and fashion tendencies.

The Lise Charmel brand can be summed up in one word: fabrics. From fine silks, guipure, and Calais laces to soft tulle and intricate floral embroideries, its innovative textile technologies and color combinations are what set it apart.

The company is rounded out by three other brand names: Antinéa, which focuses on corsetry, Éprise for the full-cup customer, and the young and vibrant Antigel line.

LOU Paris

www.lou-paris.com

Known for revolving around a new theme every season, LOU Paris encompasses the same couture-like details and glamor that are often reserved for the ready-to-wear catwalks. It comes as no surprise then that founder Lou Faller started to design and sew her own lingerie at the tender age of sixteen.

The marriage of fashion, lingerie, and fine lacework is paramount in this brand and is seen in stunning details, such as embroidered tulle and leaver's lace layered over ultrafine knit. But LOU Paris is probably best characterized by its cheeky themes and whimsical styling. The brand's signature Idole de Lou collection is dubbed "a feminine take on the tuxedo," while Clin d'Oeil thumbs its nose at convention with bow-embroidered pockets on the briefs and a flower brooch placed asymmetrically on the bra. This is a brand that is geared to the lingerie insider.

Rigby & Peller

13 Kings Road, London, SW3 4RP

Tel: +44 (0)845 076 5545, www.rigbyandpeller.com

EXPERT *Essential* As the official corsetieres to Queen Elizabeth II, Rigby & Peller has long been recognized as a company that upholds the values of craftsmanship, luxury, and exclusivity. Having started as a bespoke lingerie brand in 1939, Rigby & Peller has grown into a lingerie empire and counts some of the world's most recognizable screen and pop stars among its clientele, as well as a host of Royals. Mesh tulle, ribbon and crystal trims, delicate embroidery, and Art Deco accents on full cup and plunge bra styles, with A to H cups, as well as an array of briefs make up the brand's lingerie offerings.

« Example of Rigby & Peller's Platinum range

LINGERIE SETS

Rigby & Peller's claim to fame extends beyond its reputation for fine fabrics and exquisite detail to its world-renowned bra-fitting service. Staff members don't use a measuring tape to fit clients because they maintain that every body shape is different; they prefer instead to have women test out a variety of styles to find the right fit. Painstaking though the process may be, owner June Kenton says she's had women proclaim their Rigby & Peller bras have changed their lives.

The brand's collection includes a full range of lingerie, as well as swimwear and the new Platinum Collection of exclusive limited-edition bras and briefs, celebrating their seventieth anniversary. They also offer a highly acclaimed bespoke lingerie service at the Knightsbridge flagship location.

Simone Pérèle

Tel: (855) 647 6373, www.simone-perele.com

When Simone Pérèle set out to establish her namesake lingerie line in 1948, she did it with one conviction in mind: women don't need to sacrifice comfort for style. With years of experience as a corsetiere at hand, Pérèle designed a number of historically significant bras for her customers, including the Sole Mio in 1960, which was the first to use stretch lace, and Pétale, the first invisible bra with no underwire and adorned with intricate embroidery and appliqué, which debuted in 1968.

Today, the Simone Pérèle label stands for luxury and quality, and includes a range specially designed for women with fuller busts that runs up to an E cup.

The collection draws inspiration from influences including Japanese origami (as seen in pleated knit details), Place Vendôme jewelers (which translates to a fine embroidered star pattern), and the elegant lines of Art Nouveau.

Since 2005, Simone Pérèle has been working with the Institut Curie to help fund breast cancer research and treatment.

UNIQUE » RARE » LITTLE-KNOWN » **ULTIMATE EXPERT**

World's most expensive bra The largest lingerie brand in the world, Victoria's Secret is as famous for its endless supply of mass-market lingerie in every style, shape, and size imaginable, as its supermodel-studded ad campaigns. Since 1999, the brand has staged an annual fashion show of epic proportions, culminating in the presentation of a very precious lingerie creation. Dubbed the Fantasy Bra and usually costing in the millions of dollars, Victoria's Secret's most remarkable set was unveiled at the 2000 show when Brazilian supermodel Gisele Bündchen donned the Red Hot Fantasy Bra, consisting of more than thirteen thousand gemstones, including three hundred karats of Thai red rubies and estimated to cost around $15 million. The bra made it into the *Guinness Book of World Records* for being the most expensive piece of lingerie ever created.

Boutiques

Blush Dessous

Rosa-Luxemburg-Str. 22, 10178, Berlin

Tel: +49 (0)30 2809 3580, www.blush-berlin.com

There's more than just European design, gorgeous fabrics, and a sensual aesthetic at the heart of Blush Dessous. There's also a girls-only ethos that lends this brand a sense of strength and empowerment. From the design to the manufacture to the marketing of her lingerie, creator Claudia Kleinert ensures women are always at the helm of her brand.

Colorful silk satin, daring mesh, and delicate Chantilly lace in classic bra and brief silhouettes make this collection utterly wearable and undeniably sexy. But Blush's bestsellers, which include luxurious silk and velvet robes, girlie baby dolls, and slinky nightgowns, prove it has all your bedroom needs covered.

Damaris

Tel: +44 (0)207 613 2213, www.damaris.co.uk

Famous for her signature peek-a-boo briefs, Damaris Evans's eponymous lingerie collection is defined by exclusive yet comfortable fabrics and avant-garde design. When the designer founded her label in 2001, she set her sights on the luxury lingerie market and saw a need for fashion-forward design. Today, in addition to her hallmark "bow knickers," which are credited with starting the "bottom cleavage" trend, the Damaris label boasts seductive fabrics and stylish details, such as snakeskin, pom-poms, and Swarovski crystals.

In 2003, Evans added the Mimi Holliday diffusion line. Geared to a younger and more budget-conscious client, Mimi Holliday is made up of cheeky and flirtatious designs in bright colorways, sexy fabrics, and whimsical details.

Handmade in London, Damaris also offers clients a bespoke service and includes a yearly capsule bikini collection.

Deborah Marquit

158 West 15th Street, New York, NY 10011

Tel: (212) 478 3092, www.deborahmarquit.com

The philosophy behind Deborah Marquit's signature fluorescent lingerie collection isn't based only on her desire to create luxurious and fun undergarments, but it also stems from the writings of Carl Jung, who believed that day-glo colors appeal to the psychosexual and collective subconscious.

Marquit has made it her hallmark, since selling her first fluorescent collection to Patricia Field in 1984, to subvert the traditional with elements of the surreal. Her designs use antique styling and fine laces and turn them on their heads with fluorescent colors and unconventional materials, such as denim and vinyl. Indeed, her fluorescent Chantilly lace glows under black light. But that's not the point, according to her; rather, at the core of her collection is a strict adherence to exquisitely constructed garments; six different machines are used to create a bra.

Words from the wise

Layla L'obatti Founder,
Between the Sheets, Inc.,
USA

» Intimate fabrications

Today's consumers increasingly base their purchasing decisions on a product's environmental footprint.

Cotton varies in impact based on harvesting methods—namely water and pesticide usage. Varieties grown organically using rainwater have the smallest footprint. Silk is produced by silk worms that spin delicate fibers for their cocoons—which may be of concern to vegan consumers. Polyester, while more durable and easily cared for than natural fibers, is petroleum-based. Its impact on the environment depends on whether it is made from virgin resources or recycled from plastic bottles or old polyester materials. Rayon is a plant-based fiber manufactured from eucalyptus, beechwood, and bamboo, among other materials. Depending on the source, it may utilize fewer natural resources and pesticides than cotton, while possessing many of the same moisture-wicking properties.

Make educated decisions and sleep easy!

The brand isn't all flash, however, and includes a pretty and delicate bridal collection, as well as pastels, black, white, and nude options in most of the fabrics, and a limited-edition lace collection that changes seasonally.

Fifi Chachnil

231 rue St Honoré, 75001, Paris

Tel: +33 (0)1 42 61 21 83, www.fifichachnil.com

The ultimate in French coquetterie, Fifi Chachnil is a brand with luxury and humor at heart. The designer holds fast to the belief that a woman is never as seductive as when she isn't trying to be, and this is reflected in the retro glamor and sweet sexiness of the line's printed tulles, gingham silk chiffons, and pastel silk satins. Rounded out with cute vintage themes, such as nautical stripes, ditsy florals, and delicate polka dots, Chachnil's beginnings as a costume designer for the French stage shine through in her lingerie.

The brand has outposts in France, London, and Tokyo—where the designer's modest styles are especially revered—and includes swimwear, perfume, gloves, and a capsule collection of retro cocktail dresses. But most delightful are the days-of-the-week briefs that come in a box of seven or a "weekend box" of two.

Jean Yu

37 Crosby Street, New York, NY 10013

Tel: (212) 226 0067, www.atelierjeanyu.com

There's an androgyny to Jean Yu's lingerie designs that makes them seem utilitarian at first, but upon closer inspection discreet elements of sexiness and playfulness poke through—quite literally—in peek-a-boo cutouts strategically placed on bras and briefs, and contrast trims that add a glamorous dimension to the pieces.

Without padding, underwire, and tricks, Yu's designs are beyond delicate in whisper-thin chiffon, silk, and charmeuse with contrast elastic trims in a basic palette of black, white, and nude. Displaying a ready-to-wear flair, she takes classic silhouettes, such as the halter bra, and renders them unconventional with a wraparound band, thus creating the most avant-garde convertible bra you've ever seen. Her sleepwear offerings are equally intriguing and range from fluid layered chiffon dresses to a barely there playsuit with a plunging back.

Kiki de Montparnasse

79 Greene Street, New York, NY 10012

Tel: (212) 965 8150, www.kikidm.com

More than a lingerie brand, Kiki de Montparnasse is a lifestyle concept surrounding intimacy. What this means is that the company puts as much effort into designing high-end bras and briefs with a naughty twist as it does into its linens, loungewear, and bath and body products, as well as its selection of intimate toys and accessories. Using exclusive imported fabrics such as leaver's lace, satin, chiffon, georgette, silk, and leather, the brand fashions sexy-sweet creations that play with seduction and humor.

Bestsellers include the molded Muse bra, which uses vintage shaping for ultimate support, and the corresponding Muse heart pant, whose elegant silk satin and sheer panels are juxtaposed with a cheeky heart-shaped back. In a nod to France's lingerie heritage, the brand also offers a five-pack set of French lesson briefs in mesh and cotton jersey screen-printed with playful *bon mots* such as "aime-moi" and "fesse-moi."

The Lake & Stars

Tel: (212) 219 3305, www.thelakeandstars.com

There's an inherent cheekiness that lies at the core of The Lake & Stars, which comes as no surprise when you consider that the brand's name is a nod to the old Victorian phrase that refers to a woman's prowess in bed. The look is clean and fluid, with vintage styling by way of soft tap shorts, high-waisted briefs, demure camisoles, pretty bralettes, and bodysuits in stretch silk, chiffon, charmeuse, cotton mesh, silk jersey, and micromesh.

But there is also an element of subversion in this collection, which features decidedly risqué crotchless tie-dye stockings and sexy garter belts. This is a brand that, like most women, should not be taken at face value.

Lascivious

Tel: +44 (0)193 224 4011, www.lascivious.co.uk

Modern, sophisticated, and sexy, Lascivious has positioned itself as a luxury brand that both empowers and seduces. Chloe Hamblen launched Lascivious in 2004 and has since built it into a globally distributed label synonymous with daring and innovation.

Silhouettes extend well beyond the usual array of bras and briefs to include outré catsuits, bodysuits, and rompers that play with transparency and body

The emancipation bodice

The wasp waist was widely regarded as the fashionable silhouette in the 1800s and was achieved by wearing tightly laced and restrictive corsets. But by the latter half of the century, doctors and social critics started to speak out about the health hazards posed by corsets. In 1881, The Rational Dress Society was founded in London to protest any form of fashion that might deform the body, especially the corset.

Thus was born the emancipation bodice, a tight, sleeveless vest that buttoned up the front and was trimmed in buttons so that petticoats could be attached. It allowed a woman to maintain a fashionable silhouette while also redistributing the weight of skirts and crinolines from the waist to the shoulders and torso.

consciousness. Using traditional and exclusive fabrics, such as stretch silk satin, tulle, chiffon, and leaver's lace, Lascivious leaves a modern stamp through cheeky details, such as bras with ruched peek-a-boo cups that reveal just enough without giving it all away. Metal zippers, fringe, and tassels round out the line's edgy and creative details.

Lascivious also includes a bridal collection and hosiery, and sells vintage one-of-a-kind kimonos from Japan.

Myla

The Village, Westfield Shopping Centre, Ariel Way, London, W12 7GF

Tel: +44 (0)208 749 9756, www.myla.com

Since its inception in 1999, the goal of Myla has been to take women from the boardroom to the bedroom by offering lingerie for every aspect of their personalities. With vintage styling at its core, Myla mixes stretch satin, silk georgette, and fine mesh with the finest French and Swiss lace to create a modern boudoir look. The brand also offers sleepwear and swimwear and has created a name for itself as being the purveyor of sleek bedroom toys created in conjunction with some of the world's leading designers.

In addition to having a long list of celebrity clients, the brand reached cult status after its lace-and-freshwater-pearl thong served as a central prop in an episode of *Sex and the City*.

Strumpet & Pink

www.strumpetandpink.com

EXPERT Essential Offering a handmade collection of silk briefs, Strumpet & Pink takes fantastical themes and exquisite creativity to the limit. Founded in 2002 by artists Melanie Probert and Lisa Z Morgan, its focus is only on bottoms since the duo never actually set out to design a lingerie collection but wanted to create intimate pieces of wearable art.

Every design starts with the concept of the flower—beauty, fragility, sexuality, and joy—and is fashioned from pure silk crepe, chiffon, satin, and tulle. The briefs are cut on the bias so as to gently contour the body, and invite exploration with discreet cutouts and openings delicately adorned with pearls, ribbons, and ruffles.

The duo's creations carry names such as Princess and the Pea, Garden of Delights, Lady Chatterly's Lover, and Knock-Knock, which accentuate the lavishness and opulence of their designs: think high-waisted silk panties with columns of cascading ruffles or sheer chiffon briefs trimmed with bright rosettes and ribbons. To cap off the romantic, playful nature of their briefs, each pair comes with a hand-printed calling card in lieu of a label sewn into the garment.

« Garden of Delights underwear, by Strumpet & Pink

Designers

3.1 Phillip Lim Initials

115 Mercer Street, New York, NY 10012

Tel: (212) 334 1160, www.31philliplim.com

Phillip Lim's design mantra is to "refine instead of define," which translates to an aesthetic that's easy, chic, and, most of all, effortless. When he decided to branch out from his ready-to-wear collection with a line of intimates, he settled on the name Initials because underwear is the initial phase in dressing every day. But the name is also a nod to the antique tradition of embroidering a woman's initials into her lingerie.

The result is a collection that harks back to classic silhouettes, such as camisoles, tank tops, chemises, and bloomers in fluid fabrics like silk and jersey. Playing with the idea of innerwear as outerwear, Lim designed a line that, as he says, can transition from the home to the street. The same chic, young, and hip aesthetic that rules his catwalks is mirrored in the Initials collection with more avant-garde pieces, such as satin playsuits and cotton harem pants.

Burberry

21–23 New Bond Street, London, W1S 2RE

Tel: +44 (0)203 367 3000, www.burberry.com

A heritage brand with history and elegance at its core, the Burberry Body collection takes the brand's iconic tartan and tweaks it according to bedroom standards. That is, the strong beige, black, and red combination is muted, softened in pastel pink and blue, or diluted in tone-on-tone antique ivory and dusty rose. Fabrics tend towards the soft and romantic—tulle, chiffon, satin, and fine cotton.

The quietly luxurious line comprises a limited selection of camisoles, bras, and briefs with delicate details and exceptional fit. A sleepwear range rounds out the collection with nightshirts, pajamas, shorts, and wrap-around robes, all in Burberry's signature tartan print.

Calvin Klein Underwear

104 Prince Street, New York, NY 10012

Tel: (877) 258 7646, www.cku.com

Employing the same sleek, all-American style direction as the rest of the designer's fashion empire, Calvin Klein Underwear is as famous for its comfort and quiet luxury as its star-studded ad campaigns. First introduced in 1983, the brand produces a new collection of basics and fashion-forward styles twice yearly.

Unfussy and elegant, the line uses fine lace, satin, and printed chiffon in its more creative offerings, along with exciting prints and bright pops of color on an otherwise signature muted palette. The line of basics is what makes Calvin Klein Underwear so revered. By using laser-cut synthetics, microfiber, and modal blends, the Seductive Comfort, Perfectly Fit, and Naked collections ensure impeccable and seamless support under even the most revealing fabrics. The brand also includes a full range of sleep and loungewear.

Donna Karan Intimates

819 Madison Ave, New York, NY 10021

Tel: (212) 861 1001, www.donnakaran.com

It comes as no surprise that the same designer who developed the groundbreaking Seven Easy Pieces collection would go on to create a line of intimates that are luxe and timeless and address a woman's every need. With the pulse of New York at the heart of its design aesthetic, Donna Karan Intimates are seductive yet comfortable, luxurious but attainable.

The "Lemon Cup" bust improver

At the turn of the twentieth century, the ideal female form took on more statuesque dimensions, and a large bust was considered sexy. Although bust enhancers were nothing new—one method involved sewing wads of cotton into the lining of dresses to give the impression of a larger bosom—they rarely replicated the natural form. Designers had to get creative. The 1890s saw the introduction of the inventive, if bizarre, "Lemon Cup" bust improver. It consisted of two cotton pouches, each containing a coiled whalebone spring encased in horsehair and stuffed into a cup-shaped pad to give the bust definition. When pinned over a corset, the springs would be automatically pushed outward by the breasts and would take on a larger and more natural shape.

Practicality and functionality take precedence in this collection of mesh, satin, and Lycra-blend basics. Elements of sexiness shine through the delicate lace trims, the cut-out details, and the sensual way in which the pieces perfectly hug and support the body.

Roberto Cavalli

Via Spiga 42, Milan, 20121

Tel: +39 (0)2 76 02 09 00, www.robertocavalli.com

The king of the animal print, Roberto Cavalli is known for infusing everything he designs with sexiness, opulence, and a dose of rock 'n' roll edge. It comes as no surprise that his lingerie collection is defined by bold leopard prints, graphic zebra stripes, seductive snakeskin effects, and dramatic beading and feather trims.

From balconette and push-up bras, briefs and thongs to sweeping robes, the collection uses a mix of upscale natural materials, such as silk and satin, and mixes them with imported lace and mesh for a look that's sexy and sweet and pure Cavalli.

« Lingerie set from Cavalli's spring/summer 2011 collection

Stella McCartney

30 Bruton Street, London, W1J 6QR

Tel: +44 (0)207 518 3100,
www.stellamccartney.com

Much like her ready-to-wear line, Stella McCartney's lingerie exudes a natural sexiness and feminine appeal. The designer credits an early interest in beautiful French slips, lace, and handiwork for inspiring her collection of luxurious everyday lingerie with a vintage twist.

Silk chiffon, crêpe de Chine, leaver's lace, sheared tulle, and silk satin are the predominant fabrics. Silhouettes are simple and elegant and products range from underwire and triangle bras, briefs and thongs to more romantic lace-trimmed satin camisoles and sleepwear sets. The brand also offers cute and quirky gift sets of days-of-the-week briefs, as well as embroidered cotton "Happy Birthday" briefs.

As with everything else McCartney designs, the line includes organic and eco-friendly elements and is free of leather and fur.

Plus-size lingerie

Chantelle

www.chantelle.com

Chantelle credits its worldwide success in the lingerie field to the sweeping appeal of the French woman. She is sensual, unique, and stylish—all words that apply to Chantelle. Established in 1876, the brand is known for having created the first elasticized corsets with the discovery of vulcanized rubber and went on to other innovations, including creating the first molded bras using microfiber in the early 1970s.

From its beginnings as a company that specialized in stretchable knits, Chantelle has been known for creating lingerie for all sizes. Today, its offerings go up to a G cup and adhere to a strict code of exquisite fabrics and chic design. Using Calais and Chantilly lace, jacquard tulle and stretch satin, the brand pays close attention to shaping the bust by creating bras to either envelope, mold, or accentuate. Chantelle's hallmark is the Africa grouping, which uses embroidery on stretch tulle to create a seductive and refined look, and comprises demi-cup, T-shirt, and molded convertible bra styles, as well as a Brazilian brief, string thong, traditional brief, and boyshort.

Conturelle Dessous

www.conturelle-dessous.com

Launched in 2005, Conturelle Dessous is an exclusive line of lingerie within the historic German-based Felina lingerie brand. It draws from the former's 125-year history and expertise in the luxury corsetry and lingerie market to provide women with delicate and beautiful styles that run from an A to an H cup, and sizes 32 to 46.

UNIQUE » RARE » LITTLE-KNOWN » **ULTIMATE EXPERT**

Dita Von Teese's corset World-famous burlesque star Dita Von Teese is known for pushing boundaries. Her signature striptease performance is as remarkable for the props it uses —a giant martini glass, for example—as for the eye-popping lingerie creations she has custom-made for her. So when approached in 2007 by the charity Clothes Off Our Back to create a one-of-a-kind corset to be auctioned off, she was more than equipped for the task.

Her creation, a striking white corset encrusted with multihued Swarovski crystals and trimmed with a large hot-pink feather tail, fetched $20,000 at the auction held at Frederick's of Hollywood's flagship boutique in Los Angeles.

Marked by an elegant aesthetic, Conturelle uses sheer tulle and macramé along with mille fleur embroidery on stretch silk satin, punctuated with sophisticated details, such as satin bows, delicate piping, and Swarovski crystals.

Thanks to the company's long-standing tradition in corsetry and dedication to innovative techniques—it was the first to introduce a bra with elasticized straps in the 1960s—Conturelle has a reputation for superior fit, support, and comfort. The brand also includes a swimwear collection.

Empreinte

www.empreinte.eu

Founded in 1946, Empreinte has made a muse of the fuller-figured woman from the outset. The company's belief is that regardless of a woman's age or size, luxury, comfort, and femininity should always be the key elements in her lingerie. All of its bras range in size from 32C to 46G.

The brand is known for consistently producing bras that garner immediate fame and devotion among its clients. Most recently, this was seen in The Shells, a delicate seamless padded bra available in a balconette and plunge style.

To ensure exceptional fit, Empreinte employs an exacting process that includes elements such as the specially researched fabric it uses for the back of bras, which doesn't stretch out; straps with limited elasticity that don't lose shape or support with wear; special construction that gives balance and reduces the yield of the fabric; and a special underwire design that

In the details

Delicate machine-made lace as
seen in the very best lingerie

» Leaver's lace

If you come across the term "leaver's lace" in your
lingerie research, you're in luxury territory. Soft,
light, and sumptuous, it is considered the crème de
la crème of lingerie fabrics. Named after the
inventor of the machine that produces it—John
Leaver—the lace is distinguished by an elaborately
intertwined design within the weave of a fabric,
creating a pattern-within-a-pattern effect on even the
most delicate of materials.

When he invented his loom in 1805, Leaver
alleviated artisans of painstaking handiwork. Today,
over a century after the loom reached extinction,
high-end manufacturers have managed to replicate it
and the delicate lace it creates, though this is also
what's responsible for the fabric's high price point.
Despite being faster than hand stitching, the
machine runs at a much slower pace than other
modern technologies, thus creating a costly and
exclusive product.

makes the figure appear slender and streamlined. The brand also includes a swimwear line.

Masquerade Lingerie

Tel: +44 (0)845 270 6222, www.masquerade-lingerie.com

Born from company CEO Anthony Power's realization that the plus-size market was in dire need of a high-end lingerie brand, Masquerade takes exclusive fabrics, such as Italian stretch satin and fine mesh, and artful embroidery and marries them to precise construction. The range includes styles such as bandeau, deep plunge, and balconette bras in D to G cups.

The continental styling of the brand draws inspiration from the elegant lines of French design and the saucy spirit of Latin America. Special details include embellished embroidery, ruffles, exaggerated bows, and ultra-shine satin for a dramatic look. Slimming basques feature prominently in the collection, as do important construction elements such as reinforced shoulder straps for extra support.

PrimaDonna

www.primadonna.eu

Dating back to 1865, PrimaDonna was originally founded in Germany as a corset company for larger-breasted women. As fashions changed so did PrimaDonna's focus, which eventually went on to produce excellently manufactured bras with luxury details, such as lace and embroidery.

Today the bra range is available in fifty-eight different size combinations, from a B up to an H cup. Each bra is handmade and then given to a test model to wear and wash for several weeks to see how the bra holds up. The model then gives her feedback on the performance of the bra to the PrimaDonna designers, who in turn use this information to develop new collections with new materials.

The collection uses stretch satin and fine lace with added fashion elements, such as Swarovski crystals to create a truly beautiful and seductive look. The classic wire bra, which offers full cup support and all-day comfort, comes in a variety of fabrics and colors, making it the brand's hallmark item and a must-have in every woman's lingerie drawer. PrimaDonna also recently added Twist, a collection of seamless lingerie in vibrant prints and colors.

Bespoke lingerie

Baby Grand

Tel: +44 (0)208 699 6826, www.babygranduk.com

This "bottom-centric" label of sweet and sensuous 1950s pin-up–inspired lingerie prides itself on being unique and exclusive. Although the company produces a limited-edition lingerie collection, its couture bespoke service is its true raison d'être.

Baby Grand sources the best fabrics from around the world—silk, tulle, crepe, satin, chiffon—and renders them even more exclusive with the addition of Swarovski crystals and custom-made silk button accents. From inception to completion, every Baby Grand piece is handmade and is delivered wrapped in the brand's signature paper. Because bottoms are its focus, the brand's signature pieces are its crystal-embellished briefs and transparent heart-embroidered briefs with silk ribbon ties.

Harlette

Tel: +44 (0)207 256 4078, www.harlette.com

Named after the audacious Harlette de Falaise, mistress to the Duke of Normandy, Harlette lingerie does away with the notions of tradition and affordability and instead ventures to ask the client how she feels and how lingerie transforms her. For founder Naomi McGill, it's about turning a fantasy into wearable art.

Harlette uses couture fabrics like crystal-beaded French lace, Italian jewel-encrusted tulle, silk, and velvet with lavish trimmings, such as marabou, and ostrich and peacock feathers, and includes luxury accessories, such as diamond-and-platinum suspender clips. Harlette also creates special-order monogram clasps in gold, silver, and platinum to match any of the brand's housecoats.

Bespoke services are available in twelve cities around the world but can also be arranged in other cities should a client have a unique request.

Hélène Ponot

Tel: +33 (0)4 67 75 24 92, www.helene-ponot.com

EXPERT *Essential* Having spent years designing lingerie for other companies, where trends and profit margins dictated what she created, Hélène Ponot decided to launch her own line of bespoke lingerie in 2003. Taking her French heritage into account and her home country's long-standing tradition for being at the forefront of luxury lingerie and design, Ponot approaches her designs from a back-to-the-basics angle.

She uses the most exclusive fabrics sourced in France

« "Mademoiselle Molière," part of the 2011 collection

and accentuates them with couture details such as feathers, fur, crystals, and gemstones. Ponot thinks of her lingerie as jewelry to enhance the female form.

The designer is dedicated to ethical production and uses nontoxic fabrics and environmentally sound techniques.

Louise Feuillère

102 rue des Dames, 75017, Paris

Tel: +33 (0)1 42 93 17 76, www.louisefeuillere.com

It doesn't get more traditional than Louise Feuillère. Customers book an initial appointment with the atelier to discuss the specifics of style, fabric, and construction of their lingerie. Several fittings are scheduled, and the final garments are delivered three weeks after the last fitting. This is old-school bespoke and the ultimate in craftsmanship.

You can choose from a long list of styles and options, including corsets, bras, briefs, garter belts, slips, camisoles, loungewear, and swimwear. The fabric choices are equally vast and range from simple and traditional cottons, silks, linens, and jerseys to fashion-forward denim and mohair, as well as luxury accents like Calais and Caudry lace, printed silk, and eyelet embroidery.

Ophelia Fancy

Tel: +44 (0)127 369 8897, www.opheliafancy.com

Flirty, cute, and irreverently tongue-in-cheek, the Ophelia Fancy label was founded in 2005 by Stevi Jelbart and Emma Sandham-King. Their design

Words from the wise

Hélène Ponot Bespoke lingerie
designer, Paris, France

» Going for bespoke

When a client comes to me for bespoke lingerie, I strive to give her the most exclusive and tailor-made service possible. Usually, we have several conversations before we set an appointment. It's important to give a client ample time to make up her mind before investing in bespoke lingerie—I don't pressure her.

Upon our first meeting, we will discuss what she is looking for, and if this lingerie is for a special occasion. Then we'll look at different styles, and I will advise her on what would suit her best. I don't like to design something totally new off the bat; I will show her different materials and fabrics and will give her some ideas of what she can have done to suit her figure. In total it takes three appointments in the atelier before the garment is fully designed— every appointment allows the client the opportunity to tweak the design as she sees fit. And I'm always available to make any changes or to refit the garment.

aesthetic is theatrical and vintage inspired, and takes its cues from the world of burlesque.

Ophelia Fancy's bespoke service, called Pretty Penny, is an invitation to explore your wildest fantasies through lingerie. The designers are passionate about creating one-of-a-kind pieces and work with satin, silk dupioni, tulle, and Swarovski crystal accents, and pepper their designs with ruffles, pleating, and ribbon details. They also offer a bridal bespoke service, where bras, briefs, corsets, garters, eye masks, hair accessories, stockings, and yes, even nipple tassels can be specially made for your special day.

» Bridal

Bridal traditions

Although most brides obsess about what they will wear on their wedding days, it is what's underneath that counts most. Because this is what's really responsible for making a woman look flawless in her gown. A bridal lingerie rule of thumb is to always wear your undergarments of choice to dress fittings to make sure the innerwear and the outerwear are in synch. Bring your shapewear with you to your gown fitting, as pulling in your stomach or imagining a sleeker behind isn't an accurate representation of the final look. Make sure that you choose something comfortable if you will be wearing it all day and not just changing into it for the wedding night, and that it matches the color of your dress.

Bridal lingerie doesn't need to be purely utilitarian, however. The beauty, as with almost everything else in life, is in the details. Delicate lace ruffles, sweet satin ribbons, and dazzling crystals can all add the necessary finishing touches to any bride's ensemble and infuse the wedding night with whimsy and distinction.

Lingerie sets

Agent Provocateur

(for details see page 33)

Agent Provocateur's usual signature mix of sensuality and decadence does not escape the brand's bridal collection. Made of Chantilly and leaver's laces, Austrian embroidery, satin, and silk chiffon adorned with bows and ruffles, styles run the gamut from discreet bras in plunge and push-up styles, thongs and briefs, to intricate corsets, basques, and sexy matching suspenders. Garters, slips, a kimono, and a Wedding Set, consisting of a tulle thong with matching nipple pasties and a blindfold, mean AP has all your wedding night needs covered.

Ell & Cee

Tel: +44 (0)798 054 6245, www.ellandcee.co.uk

EXPERT Essential When Laura Cloke set out to establish the Ell & Cee lingerie collection, she did it with the idea that some lingerie is too sumptuous

« "Peek-a-boo," part of the Ell & Cee bridal range

and romantic to hide under clothes. Hence her heartbreakingly beautiful and delicate lingerie pieces—in silk chiffon, satin, and tulle, with lace and silk ribbon accents—are perfect for peeking out of a dress or blouse.

Her bridal range is equally romantic, with layers of sheer chiffon trimmed in sweet rosettes and accented with gorgeous silk bows. Brides the world over are attracted to Ell & Cee's soft satin and chiffon briefs adorned with crystals across the back that spell out The Mrs. and Just Married. There's also a bespoke option that allows you to personalize a pair of briefs by having your name or phrase of choice embroidered on the back.

Enamore

www.enamore.co.uk

Born from founder Jenny Ambrose's love for vintage sewing patterns and charismatic fabrics, Enamore was launched in 2004 in the UK. Decidedly retro, unabashedly girlie, and inspired by the 1950s pin-up, Enamore is more than just a cheeky lingerie brand. Ambrose and her team are committed to upholding strict environmental standards by using only the finest organic cotton, bamboo, soya, hemp, and natural silk. Most of the lingerie is manufactured locally, and any excess fabric is donated to local design schools and colleges.

The Blushing Brides collection is the perfect accent for the retro lover. Made of soft organic silk and trimmed in English lace, the grouping of underwire bras, ruffled panties, and camisoles comes complete with lace eye masks and bow-accented nipple pasties. In addition, any look can be accessorized with one-of-a-kind items, such as vintage-inspired cocktail hats, combs, barrettes, hair clips, corsages, and chokers handmade by one of Enamore's designers.

UNIQUE » RARE » LITTLE-KNOWN » **ULTIMATE EXPERT**

Vintage seams There are several indicators of whether something is a true vintage item or if it's just vintage-inspired, and the seams are one of them. Pinked seams, distinguished by their zigzag edges, which can be done with a sewing machine or with pinking shears, were used on woven fabrics, such as rayon and acetate, to prevent fraying. Most mass-produced slips made before 1950 used pinked seams, while high-end items used French seams, which tuck in the raw ends of excess fabric, leaving a clean look.

Material is also a good indicator of the era. Silk was always a popular choice in quality lingerie made during the first half of the twentieth century, particularly silk crepe and silk habotai in the 1920s.

Fleur of England

Tel: +44 (0)117 970 6701,
www.fleurofengland.com

Pretty, girlie, and sweet, Fleur of England (formerly known as Fleur T) is the perfect go-to label for a lingerie ensemble to make you feel complete on your wedding day. Although Fleur of England doesn't have a bridal collection per se, groupings such as Something Blue, which mixes cloudberry lace and diamond tulle with satin accents for a retro cabaret look, have a distinctly bridal appeal. Powder Puff, a romantic soft-pink satin-and-georgette grouping and the elegant cream silk-and-lace New Daisy Dreams are also suitable for brides. For something demurely sexy, try the Starlet Love Heart Brief, with a lace heart-shaped cutout in the back.

« Example set of the Powder Puff range from Fleur of England

Fred & Ginger

Tel: +44 (0)207 193 9829,
www.fred-and-ginger.com

Taking the spirit of Old Hollywood glamor—the brand is named after two of the silver screen's most iconic actors, after all—and mixing it with modernity and edge, Fred & Ginger is a sophisticated, luxurious, and sexy collection of lingerie, nightwear, and boudoir accessories.

The brand's bridal offerings are the epitome of classic seduction. French silk satin and Chantilly lace bras are accented with large, dramatic satin bows and paired with ruffled briefs and silk tap shorts. A corset, negligée, teddy, chemise, suspenders, kimono robe, and garter round out the collection.

Gilda & Pearl

Tel: +44 (0)753 050 9335, www.gildapearl.co.uk

With femininity, empowerment, and desirability at its core, Gilda & Pearl creates one-of-a-kind garments for the lingerie connoisseur. Designer Diane Houston handcrafts each item, ensuring that each piece is unique, while also giving her customers the option to make modifications to their favorite styles. Gilda & Pearl takes satin, chiffon, and English lace and blends them in unconventional ways to create pieces that are at once softly beautiful and daringly edgy.

Chiffon, silk, lace, and satin feature prominently in the label's bridal offerings. The collection is romantic and beautiful, and marked by a distinctly vintage flair that includes ruffles, large silk bows, and coordinated garters.

La Perla

(for details see page 35)

For the couture bride there really is no other choice than La Perla. Defined by the brand's reputation for luxury, opulence, and exclusivity, the bridal collection offers an extensive selection of styles and silhouettes ranging from the practical to the extravagant.

Leaver's lace, silk georgette, satin, and macramé are mixed and manipulated to create standout items, such as a sweeping lace robe, a striking intricate stretch lace body, and a demure convertible bustier with delicate lace panels on the back.

The bridal trousseau

From the Old French *trousse*, meaning bundle, the bridal trousseau was a collection of lingerie, linens, jewelry, and accessories that a young woman would accumulate for the start of her new life. Traditionally, this also included new dresses and ensembles for her wedding night, her honeymoon, and her early years as a newlywed. These items were handmade either by the bride's mother and aunts, or wealthier families commissioned them to a seamstress. In Marguerite Bentley's 1947 book *Wedding Etiquette Complete*, she breaks down lingerie trousseau essentials to three groupings: the wedding night, nightgowns and slips, and everyday items. She describes the latter as "beautiful tailored sets in flat crépe, often monogrammed and bound in another color."

Marie Jo

17 rue de la Bourse, Lille, 59000

Tel: +33 (0)3 20 14 59 45, www.mariejo.com

Exacting standards and exquisite quality are the hallmarks of Marie Jo. Every piece of lingerie undergoes consumer testing before it is put into production. And once it makes it into a new collection, it is assembled in over thirty different procedures, ensuring a perfectly constructed design. As if that weren't enough, once completed, each garment goes through two more manual inspections. It's a rigorous process that dates back to the brand's origins as the Van de Velde Belgian corset company in 1919.

Marie Jo's bridal offerings are the pinnacle of elegance. Ultrafine tulle embroidery inspired by Russian grandeur, pretty piqué with delicate scalloped edges, and bold contemporary floral embellishments in a range of colors—because there's more to your wedding day than just white—in an extensive range of silhouettes means there's something for practically everyone.

Rigby & Peller

(for details see page 40)

With glamor and sophistication at its core, Rigby & Peller offers the Vintage range of bridal lingerie, with romantic touches reminiscent of a bygone era. Fine floral embroidery on mesh tulle, Swarovski crystal embellishments, and satin-covered buttons add delicate details to the plunge, full cup, and balcony bras and bikini, thong, and brief pants. The most noteworthy style of the collection, however, is the high-waisted ruffle pant that blends discreet seduction with retro charm.

Valisere

www.valisere.com

The high-end brand within Germany's stalwart Triumph International stable, Valisere's history dates back to 1913, when it was founded in France by Auguste Perrin. It started as an offshoot of the Le Grand Perrin leather glove company and still maintains a heritage approach to luxury fabric and craftsmanship today.

Valisere's bridal offerings draw from retro glamor and understated seduction to create pieces such as an Empire-style corset with floral motif and Swarovski crystal beading and a soft bustier with delicate embroidery and detachable garters. For something a little more risqué, opt for the Affaire Discrete set, comprising a ribbon-tie thong, nipple tassels, and handcuff accessories.

Garters

A tradition dating back to sixteenth-century France, when the wedding party visited the newlywed couple in their chambers after consummation, a groomsman would take a piece of the bride's clothing for luck—usually one of the garters she wore to hold up her stockings. He would then wear it in his hat for the remainder of the festivities.

Changing traditions

By the nineteenth century, tradition dictated that the bride remove her own garter during the celebration and toss it to the groomsmen. As rowdier weddings would sometimes result in impatient men taking it upon themselves to remove the bride's garter, the tradition was once again tweaked and the sole responsibility of removing the garter and tossing it to the bachelors in attendance was given to the bridegroom.

Today, as the garter-toss tradition continues, most designers sell their creations in twos: a simple garter to be thrown to the men during the party and a more intricate design that can be stored as a keepsake for the bride.

Florrie Mitton

· www.florriemitton.com

EXPERT Essential Naming her brand after her great grandmother and with a deep reverence for all things vintage and exquisite, Claire Quigley

<< "Je t'aime" lace garter
by Florrie Mitton

launched the Florrie Mitton label of couture wedding garters on Etsy when the search for her own proved futile. Her range is now available from numerous suppliers. As if thumbing her nose at the lack of options in the bridal market, Quigley's designs are staggeringly beautiful and look as though they belong behind glass, not under a dress.

Her simple silk garters are as delicately stunning as her more avant-garde creations, such as bursts of soft tulle with delicate embroidery and tiered lace trimmed in satin and pearls. Lace ruffles, scalloped edges, hand embellishment, beads, and crystal details make this one garter you'll never want to toss.

Laura George

Tel: +44 (0)753 465 2282, www.laurageorge.co.uk

Elegant and glamorous, Laura George's bridal garters, made from fine antique laces, tulle, and silk, and adorned with satin bows, pearls, and Swarovski crystals, are the perfect finishing touch for any bride. The designer brings ten years of experience in the lingerie arena to her eponymous endeavor. The vast array of garters ranges from the simple and sophisticated, such as white lace designs with blue ribbon accents, to the truly exclusive, adorned with detachable diamond, sapphire, and ruby charms that can be later strung on a necklace. George also makes limited-edition pieces and takes bespoke orders.

Ossai

Tel: (510) 209 6998,
www.ossaibridalaccessories.com

Necessity served as the mother of invention for Zalikha Safdari—known as Ossai to her friends and family—who found the bridal market was in dire need of artful and original accessories while planning her own wedding. Drawing from the expert techniques she learned from her mother and her niece's know-how as a fashion school graduate, Ossai founded her eponymous label of garters, hairpieces, sashes, and veils with the idea of family and love at the core.

Her garters are at once ethereal and opulent. Antique lace, satin, and silk designs are adorned with crystals, pearls, paillettes, and semi-precious stones for a unique and modern spin on a traditional accessory item.

The Garter Girl by Julianne Smith

Tel: (202) 607 3683, www.thegartergirl.com

When Julianne Smith was tasked with finding her friend a garter for her wedding day, she was determined to fulfill her one and only bridesmaid responsibility with aplomb. Unfortunately, it was next to impossible to meet her friend's request for something "furry." Harboring a love for crafts and do-it-yourself design, Smith took it upon herself to design a garter for her friend and quickly parlayed it into The Garter Girl.

Her offerings are divided into several categories— traditional, modern, eco-friendly, something blue, and couture—and use satin, lace, grosgrain, feathers, and beads in innovative and original ways. Smith also creates custom designs upon request.

The chastity belt

Despite its medieval associations—and its continued parody in television and films— historical analysis has shown that there is little probability chastity belts were in existence during the Crusades, as metalworking techniques of the time were too rudimentary to craft an undergarment for long-term use.

In fact, although metal chastity belts were used as far back as Renaissance Italy, they were far from ubiquitous and not nearly as misogynistic as you might think. They were agreed upon in mutual consent of both man and woman, and were used to curb temptation as well as reduce the possibility of sexual abuse or rape. More often than not, however, the chastity belt was a concept perpetuated by literature and myth.

» Corsetry

Evolution of the corset

From torture to titillation, the corset stands as one of the most enduring symbols of femininity. Art and artifacts tell us that corsets (also known as stays) date back to Ancient Greece, when women would cinch their waists with a thick leather band in order to accentuate their busts, thus propagating the notion of their fertility to men.

Corsets didn't come back into fashion until the sixteenth century, when the inverted cone shape that was the desirable silhouette of the time called for a stiffened garment that would flatten the breasts while pushing them up so that they almost "spilleth over." This look dominated for the next two centuries.

Victorian corsets

The Victorian Age ushered in the hourglass silhouette and the corset's reputation for being a torture device that restricted breathing and induced fainting, as well as reports of causing deformity and even death. Because fashion had shifted its focus to the waist and the look of shoulders had softened, the only way to achieve the new hourglass silhouette was by whittling the midsection as much as possible.

This gave birth to the practice of tightlacing, where a corset's laces are pulled as tightly as possible to achieve a considerably reduced waist—remember Vivien Leigh grasping on to the bedpost as her maid tightened her corset in *Gone With The Wind?* Reports vary wildly on how much reduction can be achieved with a corset, but most women manage to shave off no more than a few inches. Tightlacing is still practiced today, although it is often more associated with sadomasochism and fetishism.

Streamlined silhouette

Thankfully, the Roaring Twenties brought about a more streamlined silhouette that quickly gave way to soft brassieres instead of rigid corsets. And although the wasp waist came back in the late 1940s, technology swiftly ushered in elasticized girdles that sucked it in while allowing women to breathe out.

Modern corsetry

Much as the corset came to represent the oppression and subjugation of women, no other garment has been able to highlight and celebrate the female form in quite the same way. It's for this reason that women still gravitate to corsets today—be they for fantasy or fashion, for the boudoir or for the bride. The corset does have periodic revivals in the world of mainstream fashion, but more often, the trend is to wear it as outerwear. Although modern corsets have features reminiscent of traditional corsetry, such as lacing and boning, they don't actually have much effect on your body shape.

Corset style guide

There are a few different styles of corsets, of which these are the most common:

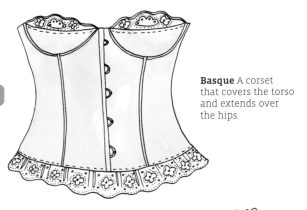

Basque A corset that covers the torso and extends over the hips.

Bustier A short shaping garment that covers the breasts but stops at the waist; it is not usually boned.

Overbust A corset that covers the torso from just under the arms to the hips.

Underbust A corset that starts just under the breasts and extends to the hips.

Waist cincher (or guepière) A shorter corset that starts on the lower rib cage and extends to just above the hips.

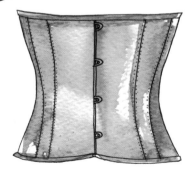

Corsetiers

Cadolle

4 rue Cambon, 75001, Paris

Tel: +33 (0)1 42 60 94 22, www.cadolle.com

Five generations of Cadolle women have upheld and continue to perpetuate this brand's reputation for precision, innovation, and style. Founded in the late nineteenth century by Herminie Cadolle, a pioneering businesswoman who initially established the company in Buenos Aires before returning to Paris at the beginning of World War I. Cadolle has a long list of trailblazing credits: the company was the first to incorporate rubber in corset construction, and by cutting the traditional corset in half and selling it as a top and bottom support garment, Herminie was arguably the first to design the modern bra. (Although Mary Phelps Jacob would certainly have a thing or two to say about that!)

Today Cadolle produces a ready-to-wear lingerie line of bras, briefs, bustiers, and corsets, but the company is renowned for its custom creations of all kinds of lingerie, including corsets and bridal gowns. A one-on-one appointment in Cadolle's Paris atelier is necessary, as are at least one to three fittings before the garment is finalized.

Dark Garden

321 Linden Street, San Francisco, CA 94102

Tel: (415) 431 7684, www.darkgarden.com

Founded in 1989, the Dark Garden team, headed by Autumn Adamme, creates corsets and wedding gowns that truly express each individual's personality and style—bringing out her natural beauty and boosting her confidence. Blending old-world techniques with up-to-the-minute information, the designers produce garments that flatter and fit with amazing comfort. Dark Garden offers more than ten styles of ready-to-wear corsets in fourteen sizes as well as a vast array of custom-made styles—all made from the finest-quality silks, laces, and leathers.

The company's exceptional attention to detail and eye for design, in addition to their focus on comfort and customer connection, have led to a dedicated following, catching the eye of a number of celebrities, such as Christina Aguilera, Kelly Osbourne, Pamela Anderson, Marilyn Manson, and Dita Von Teese.

Ender Legard Corsetry

Tel: +44 (0)783 424 4481,
www.enderlegardcorsetry.com

EXPERT *Essential* When Asia Smaga unveiled her first limited-edition collection of couture corsets in 2003, Browns Bride snatched them up instantly. Her name quickly became synonymous with luxury and fine craftsmanship, and she launched her Ender Legard label two years later. It comes as no surprise that Smaga, who was born in Poland but is based in London, would have gone down the sartorial path, considering she spent her formative years working in her aunt's corsetry studio.

Especially regarded for her bridal corsets of exquisite guipure lace, stretch silk satin, intricate pleating and embroidery, and delicate pearl straps, Smaga also designs a ready-to-wear lingerie collection that is marked for its expert tailoring and flawless shaping abilities.

Kunza Corsetiere

www.corsetorium.com

When Kunza sets about creating one of her unique corsets, she considers history and tradition before anything else. Classically trained at Vivienne Westwood, she has created one-of-a-kind corsets for the likes of Keira Knightley, Helen Mirren, and Elizabeth Hurley, as well as the fashion houses of Dolce & Gabbana and Roberto Cavalli.

The ultimate goal of a Kunza corset is to celebrate the female form by fashioning timeless pieces, which the designer achieves by using original Victorian laces, trimmings, and silks for an array of classic and intricate designs. She uses modern pattern-cutting techniques to ensure a perfect fit and incorporates some cutting-edge designs into her repertoire, such as laser-cut

Words from the wise

Autumn Adamme Founder,
Dark Garden Unique Corsetry,
San Francisco, CA

» The right corset

Whether worn for support or seduction, modern corsets offer nipped waists, lifted bosoms, sculpted hips, and, when purchased from an experienced corset maker, far more comfort and much greater sex appeal than today's elasticized, all-in-one underwear.

When shopping for a corset, be sure to look for steel (never plastic) boning, short stitches, lining, and—believe it or not—enough space to breathe. These complicated garments work best when they're sized by measuring the waist; most often the corset measurement will be about four inches smaller. Better still are corsets that are custom made by a corsetiere who offers at least one mock-up fitting to insure a proper fit through the length as well as circumference of the body.

Beware of "corsets" that are sized small, medium, or large; they rarely create the ultra-feminine curves that are easily achieved with gentle waist reduction.

leather cinchers. Her made-to-measure service is highly exclusive and can only be arranged by appointment in her London atelier, but she also sells a small selection of corsetry to a few boutiques worldwide.

Mr. Pearl

Fax: +33 (0)1 53 10 85 62

EXPERT *Essential* Perhaps one of the fashion industry's most elusive personalities, Mr. Pearl is widely regarded as the best bespoke corsetier in the world. True haute couture in every sense, Mr. Pearl has created corsets for Christian Lacroix, Jean Paul Gaultier, and Thierry Mugler, as well as private clients, such as Dita Von Teese, Kylie Minogue, and Victoria Beckham, who wore a custom design under her wedding dress in 1999 and had the designer on hand to lace her into it.

Mr. Pearl's creations can take months to complete and require numerous fittings. He himself wears a corset twenty-four hours a day, seven days a week, and reportedly takes it off only to bathe—he says he does this to empathize with his clients. His atelier is nestled behind Notre Dame cathedral in Paris, but he's a staunch

« Back view of one of Mr. Pearl's creations

opponent to technology and doesn't have a website or email address. The only way to contact him is via fax.

Puimond Progressive Corset Design

Tel: (323) 650 4891, www.puimond.com

Not for the shy, Puimond's corsets marry traditional techniques with edgy style — that's probably why he's been commissioned for custom creations by envelope-pushing personalities, such as Madonna and American sex symbol Marnie Van Doren. He is passionate about details and originality and is known for his elaborate custom waist-nipping pieces. He uses a patterned hourglass waistline form with extra curvature over the rib cage and hips that makes for a

The farthingale

In the sixteenth century, Spanish fashion exerted its influence on the dress of the English and Italian courts. The predominant silhouette of the time was an inverted cone shape that flattened the bust and ended in a tiny waistline, with voluminous skirts to accentuate the hips. In order to achieve this, a graduated hooped crinoline, called the Spanish farthingale, came into favor. Its hoops were made of wood or whalebone, and it attached itself to the bottom hem of the corset, weighing women down and forcing them to move much slower and more carefully, resulting in the elegant sashay they adopted.

more comfortable fit with less pressure placed on the torso. High-end leather, lacings, and heavy stitching mean the corsets can withstand tightlacing techniques. All of his designs are lined in English cotton Coutil for comfort, and fabric choices range from satin and brocade to PVC and leather. Custom creations take three to four weeks.

UNIQUE » RARE » LITTLE-KNOWN » **ULTIMATE EXPERT**

The diamond thong At the 2008 Singapore Fashion Festival underwear brand Triumph International pulled out all the stops in presenting its new collection of lingerie, inspired by powerful and mythical women of the past. The company staged a lingerie fashion show called Viva la Eve that culminated in the unveiling of a diamond-encrusted thong valued at approximately $130,000. Inspired by the Garden of Eden, the thong comprised 518 diamonds (worth 30 karats) and was trimmed in 27 white gold tassels. It was created by Singapore's Lee Hwa Jewelry and took more than two months to make. It made its runway debut on a Romanian model carried down the catwalk on the shoulders of two male models.

Velda Lauder Corsetiere

Tel: +44 (0)207 281 5623, www.veldalauder.co.uk

Velda Lauder went through a few transformations before settling as a bespoke and ready-to-wear corsetier, including designing clothing for rock stars and royalty and working as a stylist for *Tatler*. It wasn't until 1997 that she first introduced corsetry to her designs, and she was instantly hooked. Since then she's created a collection of corsets for international luxury lingerie boutique Coco de Mer; her designs have been featured in music videos; and she has collaborated on the world famous Victoria's Secret fashion show. Her designs use duchess satin, silk, lace, feathers, and Swarovski crystals and are styled for bridal, burlesque, or classic use. Lauder passed away in 2013, and though the future of her label is uncertain, she has left an important and memorable legacy behind.

Mane Lange

Hagenauer Strasse 13, 10435 Berlin

Tel: +49 (0)30 4432 8482, www.manelange.de

Specializing in corsetry and bridal gowns, Mane Lange is a go-to destination for exquisitely ornate corsets in a charming couture environment. Printed silks and satins, elaborate brocades, and even the odd religious motif sum up Lange's classic-meets-contemporary approach to corset design. Whether you seek something custom made or just custom fit, these designs can take you down the aisle as easily and stylishly as they can down the street.

In the details

The different materials used to
create the structure of a corset,
from whalebone to plastic

» Steel and bones

During the sixteenth to the eighteenth centuries,
corsets were heavily boned using whalebone or giant
reeds, perennial canes native to eastern and southern
Asia. The busk, which is the rigid element that runs
down the front of the corset and holds its structure,
was made of wood or bone, often decorated or
inscribed.

By the late nineteenth century, a new hourglass
silhouette called for more complex boning, and the
growing price of whalebone forced designers to
explore other options. Cork strips, cording, and
featherbone were all viable alternatives, but steel was
the most ubiquitous material. As comfort started to
take precedence in the corset design of the early
twentieth century, flexible spiral steel boning
replaced its original rigid counterpart. Today, most
corsets use nylon or plastic boning, although luxury
ones use only steel: either flat, which bends in one
direction, or spiral, which bends in two directions.

Designers

Jean Paul Gaultier

44 avenue George V, 75008 Paris

Tel: +33 (0)1 44 43 00 44,
www.jeanpaulgaultier.com

From creating Madonna's iconic cone-busted silhouettes for her Blond Ambition tour to his first eponymous fragrance bottled in corseted glass, Jean Paul Gaultier has established himself as one of haute couture's preeminent corsetiers. Less an homage to tradition than a statement on futuristic, urban warriors, Gaultier's corseted couture and ready-to-wear creations have become his stamp on fashion and draw from historical technique with modern twists, such as braided dégradé taffeta and basket-weave silk. He has created designs for several films, including a television version of the period drama *Liaisons Dangereuses* starring Catherine Deneuve, and has collaborated with La Perla Black Label for a limited collection of luxury corsets and bustiers.

Peter Soronen

www.petersoronen.com

Early in his career, Chicago-born Peter Soronen was obsessed with the corseted shape and used vintage corset patterns in his designs with complex boning and seaming. Even now, as his obsession has grown into a fully fledged designer label based in New York, Soronen still focuses on the waist and is as inspired by the Victorian and Elizabethan eras as the 1950s. His designs celebrate the hourglass figure with curve-hugging patterns in bold-colored brocades, silks, and plaids with hand appliqué, embroidery, and contrast piping. It's no wonder he is favored by the elegant and distinctive First Lady Michelle Obama, in addition to a host of A-list celebrities.

Vivienne Westwood

44 Conduit Street, London, W1S 2YL

Tel: +44 (0)207 439 1109,
www.viviennewestwood.com

Punk princess, maven of the anti-establishment, perpetuator of chaos: it's hard to believe that the

The Merry Widow of lingerie

In 1952, as the operetta *The Merry Widow* was being reinterpreted for the silver screen starring Lana Turner, the Warner's lingerie company released a corresponding undergarment. It featured demi-cups and a short girdle that stopped just above the thigh and had long garters attached along the trim to hook on to stockings. It was steel-boned and had slim panels of black elastic netting and a zipper inserted behind the hook-and-eye busk. Turner famously remarked: "I'm telling you, the Merry Widow was designed by a man. A woman would never do that to another woman."

same woman who introduced the Sex Pistols to the world has also gone on to enjoy a prolific career as a fashion designer, marked for celebrating history and tradition in her designs. Westwood is credited with introducing the first modern corset as outerwear on the catwalk as part of her Harris Tweed collection in 1987. Her corsets, which have figured prominently in her designs since the late 1980s, are historically accurate and feature modern practicalities, such as elastic fabrication and removable sleeves. The structure of the corset still finds its way into her creations today and makes up the foundation of many of her celebrated tailored separates.

» Extras

Extras and accessories

Winding down and turning in have the kind of soporific connotations that inspire the desire for comfort and fluidity. But whether you're a negligée kind of lady or a men's pajamas kind of gal, there's no excuse for sloppy nightwear. From an aesthetic standpoint, it always feels good to look good (and who knows, maybe it will even help you sleep better). From a wellness perspective, well-made garments in natural fabrics are healthier and more beneficial. Thankfully, there are designers who strive to bring back the days of elegance in every state of your life, even your dream state.

As for your wind-down, luxe fabrics and fashion-forward silhouettes can be so much more comfortable than an old pair of sweatpants. You could argue that it is considerably easier to decompress in cashmere, or that lounging is a more attractive pursuit in a fluid dress or an edgy jumpsuit. Indeed women have been known to entertain in silky lounge pants and velvet slippers. It says: "Welcome to my home, kick back, and stay for a while."

Nightwear and loungewear

Argentovivo

Via Farini 10/A, Bologna

Tel: +39 (0)51 265 404,
www.argentovivofashion.it

EXPERT Essential Sexy and luxurious, Argentovivo's collection of lingerie, sleepwear, and loungewear is the ultimate in sophistication. Delicate camisoles, slinky chemises, and elegant nightwear use only the best pure silk and mercerized cotton trimmed in Calais and Chantilly lace and are highlighted with couture accents, such as intricate hand embroidery and ribbon detail. Panels of mesh are soft and breathable and lend a daring aesthetic. Robes and loungewear separates are chic and cozy in mohair, cashmere, and Merino wool fabrications with ruched and pleated details.

Ari Dein

Tel: (212) 929 7524, www.aridein.com

Arielle Shapiro, founder of Ari Dein, has a storied fashion background that dates back to the 1930s, when her grandparents owned an exclusive fur company in Manhattan. But it wasn't until the art history graduate moved to Florence to study fashion that her history affected her present. She uses the old Art Deco New York of the 1920s as inspiration for her collection of chemises, gowns, camisoles, robes, and briefs. Her designs carry names, such as

» Mercerized cotton

Mercerized cotton (also known as pearl cotton) undergoes a chemical process that alters the fiber's structure and makes it more resilient, lustrous, softer, easier to dye, and less prone to shrinkage. The process is named after John Mercer, who devised it in 1844 when he treated cotton fibers with sodium hydroxide. This made the fabric stronger and easier to dye but also shrank it, thus making it an unattractive prospect to manufacturers. It wasn't until Horace Lowe tweaked the process in 1890—by holding the fabric during treatment to prevent shrinkage—that he found that by applying tension to the cotton it also gained luster and light-reflecting properties.

The process is still used today, although with the addition of an acid bath. The resulting fabric has the same qualities, but is also more prone to attracting lint. For this reason, cotton with long staple fibers in its raw form responds best to mercerization.

Boutique Hotel—contrast Art Deco–inspired trim on a silk charmeuse chemise, camisole, shorts, and gown—and AD Vintage—muted floral-print chiffon with black piping on a hooded peignoir, camisole, and shorts. Shapiro is committed to supporting the local manufacturing industry, and each piece is made exclusively in New York.

Between the Sheets

Tel: (347) 688 2008, www.btslingerie.com

Luxurious in its simplicity, the Between the Sheets collection is an understated mix of intimates and loungewear. Founded by Layla L'obatti in 2010 alongside her racier namesake label with the tagline "Specimens of Seduction," these two ranges deliver everything a luxury nightwear consumer is looking for. The BTS collection features sensuous designs from a feminine perspective, while L'obatti's luxe range boasts decadent silk with artful lace appliqués that bring a touch of vintage glamor to modern lingerie design.

Bodas

43 Brushfield Street, London, E1 6AA

Tel: +44 (0)207 655 0958, www.bodas.co.uk

Mix and match is the Bodas philosophy. A full range of lingerie, nightwear, and loungewear, with some beachwear thrown in the mix, Bodas is the perfect solution to any style dilemma, with its clean lines and minimalist styling. This collection of luxurious basics comes in the finest Swiss and Supima mercerized cottons and features a range of classic loungewear, such as nightshirts, men's pajamas, camisoles, shorts, and kimono robes. Shadow stripes and classic check patterns are the ultimate in chic, while brushed cotton and jersey make these pieces you'll never want to take off.

Carine Gilson

87 rue A. Dansaert, B-1000 Brussels

Tel: +32 (0)2 289 51 47, www.carinegilson.com

EXPERT *Essential* Sleek, simple, and elegant, Carine Gilson's designs can easily double as outerwear but cast an undeniably chic shadow when worn as lingerie.

Gilson's fabric of choice is natural silk—whose innate luminescence adds to the designs' sophisticated and fluid appeal—along with touches of lace, satin, and silk chiffon. Silhouettes are basic, comprising a full range of bra and brief styles, as well as bodysuits, camisoles, slips, and chemises with delicate dévoré floral details, scalloped edges, and exquisite embroideries done by artisans in her Brussels atelier.

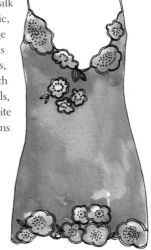

» Carine Gilson winter 2010/2011 collection

Hanro

Tuchlauben 13, 1010 Vienna

Tel: +43 (0)1 533 9305, www.hanro.com

Founded in Switzerland in 1884, Hanro has a long tradition of providing customers with some of the most exclusive and comfortable loungewear, sleepwear, and underwear on the market. Using the finest mercerized Swiss cotton and embroidery exclusively developed for the brand, as well as French guipure and leaver's lace, Hanro creates a varied selection of basic and fashion nightwear and loungewear. Soft, fluid, and sophisticated, details include elegant pleating, discreet embroidery, and understated design. The brand's loungewear pieces are especially comfortable in micromodal and silk blends, and additional considerations, such as extra-broad waistbands on yoga pants, make them perfect for travel.

Jonquil

www.jonquillingerie.com

Old Hollywood glamor is in Jonquil designer Diane Samandi's blood. Her fashion illustrator grandmother and silent-film-star great aunt together instilled in her the ideals of vintage charm and sophisticated design. Samandi started her design career in the 1970s with patchwork bikinis, which quickly graduated to dresses and finally to a luxury lingerie and loungewear line in 1980. Today her collection consists of romantic sweeping chemises and robes in silk satin and printed chiffon, trimmed in embroidered mesh and antique lace. Samandi also designs a younger loungewear and daywear collection called In Bloom by Jonquil that mixes a fresh, flirty aesthetic with technical materials.

Leigh Bantivoglio

www.leighbantivoglio.com

A delicate lace fan acts as Leigh Bantivoglio's insignia, and nothing could be more indicative of her soft, romantic, and dreamy creations. Her collection of camisoles, chemises, robes, and lingerie separates uses delicate bias-cut silk satin and intricate French lace and comes accented with detailed ribbons and bows. The designer strives to empower women from the inside out with her creations, because wearing them "is like having your

Nightcaps

A nightcap was a long piece of cloth that women wrapped around their heads before going to bed. Its original purpose was to safeguard against head lice. For wig wearers, who generally had little or no hair, nightcaps were especially useful as lice would propagate in the wig. The nightcap would keep what little hair they had from being infested. On a more aesthetic note, women also wore nightcaps to keep their natural hairstyles in place while they slept.

own little secret," according to her. Soft pastels and bold jewel tones are trimmed in exquisite antique lace on such outerwear-worthy silhouettes as wraparound camisoles and chemises that could easily double as cocktail dresses.

Patricia Fieldwalker

Tel: (604) 689 1210, www.pfieldwalker.com

Combining European elegance with North American energy, Patricia Fieldwalker's pieces have appeared on Julia Roberts in *Pretty Woman* and Glenn Close in *Fatal Attraction*—exactly the type of strong female personalities she designs for. Contemporary, fresh, and sensuous, her collection uses silk charmeuse, cotton, velvet, and Calais and leaver's laces, on classic chemise, camisole, and pajama silhouettes in colors ranging from soft pastels to bold berry shades.

Innerwear as outerwear

The innerwear as outerwear trend can be traced back to the beginning of time—depending on where time starts for you—to the loincloths worn by ancient Egyptians, the togas favored by the Romans and, indeed, even Adam and Eve's fig leaves. In these cases, the garments, minimal though they were, served to conceal nudity and maintain a sense of humility and decency.

Innerwear evolution

Flash forward to the latter half of the twentieth century, to artists such as Madonna taking the notion of modesty and turning it on its head with a bustier in place of a blouse and a white see-through camisole layered over a black lace bra, and innerwear as outerwear was decidedly more risqué. It wasn't long before runways and radical teens alike were wearing silky, lace-trimmed chemises as dresses and bra tops under unbuttoned plaid flannel shirts. By the time the Spice Girls hit the scene, no one batted an eyelash at Victoria Beckham's minimalist barely there dresses.

Coming and going

The trend has faded in and out of the larger fashion picture since then, but it has left an indelible mark on the industry nonetheless. We have Hervé Leger and Calvin Klein to thank – the former being responsible for the indisputably lingerie-inspired bandage dress of the 1980s and the latter for

Beckham's aforementioned 1990s era barely-there frock. And we mustn't forget Dolce & Gabbana, the purveyors of the corset dress as inspired by their unlikely muse, the Sicilian widow.

The modern trend

Today the trend persists with brands such as VPL by Victoria Bartlett, a line of undergarment-inspired clothes that first launched in 2003. Bartlett has once again turned fashion inside out, except unlike her predecessors, she doesn't do it for sensuality's sake. In fact, the VPL aesthetic adheres to the brand's mantra of functionality, comfort, and style. As Bartlett says, "I don't do T and A." Like so many trends in fashion, innerwear as outerwear has come full circle.

Bordelle

Tel: +44 (0)208 968 4488, www.bordelle.co.uk

EXPERT *Essential* It was in searching for a middle ground between outerwear and lingerie that Alexandra Popa and Javier Suarez established Bordelle in 2007. By taking the bodycon aesthetic and customizing it with a proprietary technique using satin elastic bandages, Bordelle pushes the boundaries of societal norms, drawing from

» From the fall/winter 2009/10 Bordelle collection

Words from the wise

Arielle Shapiro Founder, Ari
Dein, New York, NY

» Wearing the inside out

If you want to embrace the innerwear as outerwear
trend, start by choosing one top from your intimates
collection to style with a few favorites from the rest of
your closet. This could be a corset, a bra or a
camisole of any material. Allow the lingerie to be the
focus of the look, but be careful not to overdo it. A
lace-trimmed camisole looks lovely belted over
skinny jeans, as does a lace bralette under a sheer
patterned blouse, but keep the rest of your look
conservative and tailored or it will kill the effect.

When dressing for trends, I can't stress enough the
importance of paying close attention to your body
type. Women with fuller busts might not get away
with the same look as their less endowed sisters. That
doesn't mean you can't have fun experimenting with
layers and laces, but if you can see a nipple or you're
spilling out of your top, you've probably gone too far.

the provocative world of S&M. The resulting couture bondage dresses (that double as girdles), suspenders, bodysuits, bra and brief sets, and accessories are not for the fainthearted.

Vannina Vesperini

4 rue de Tournon, 75006 Paris

Tel: +33 (0)1 56 24 32 72,
www.vanninavesperini.com

"Visible lingerie" is what Vannina Vesperini calls her collection of molded satin bras with French lace appliqué, camisoles, and chemises that are delicate yet bold and draw inspiration from vintage silhouettes. It isn't underwear or outerwear; it is what the designer calls a "lingerie attitude."

VPL

5–7 Mercer Street, New York, NY 10013

Tel: (646) 912 6141, www.vplnyc.com

Designed by Victoria Bartlett, VPL is a line of undergarment-inspired clothes that first launched in 2003. Wanting to fill the niche between lingerie and sportswear, Bartlett mixes the utilitarianism of underwear with uniforms, bold colors, and unexpected accessories. She turns fashion inside out with playsuits, camisoles, bra tops, and bustiers that adhere to a mantra of functionality, comfort, and style.

Hosiery

Silky, smooth, and with an elegant sheen, stockings were an integral part of the overall fashion look of the sixteenth century—for men, that is. Women weren't allowed to show their legs in public until the twentieth century, which means for four hundred years, most stocking manufacture was aimed at men. The dawn of legwear was in 1589, when Reverend William Lee invented the knitting machine and made stockings out of cotton, wool, and silk for men to wear under their breeches. And while stocking production didn't change much during those four hundred years, the innovation that truly rocked the world of hosiery was the use of nylon in 1935.

Nylons

The first nylon stockings appeared in 1940 and were an instant success. On the first day alone, more than seventy-two thousand pairs were sold, collapsing the Japanese silk market virtually overnight. During World War II, nylon was an integral material in the making of parachutes and tents, making nylon stockings a hot commodity. When the war ended, fully fashioned stockings—thus named because they were tailored to suit a particular leg shape instead of the one-shape-fits-all philosophy we have now—with their distinctive seam, were all the rage. Women who couldn't afford them would draw a line up the backs of their legs to simulate the look.

Pantyhose

Pantyhose came into existence in the 1960s, when Allen Grant sewed stockings to briefs, eliminating the need for garter belts and creating a full-coverage item that could be worn under the decade's popular micro miniskirts.

Today, high-end hosiery is marked by certain characteristics, such as run-guard construction, pressure-free bands, the addition of shapewear technology, and seamless composition, as well as fashion details, such as Swarovski crystals, imported lace, intricate de-sign, and even feather trims. Noted brands include Philippe Matignon, Wolford, Falke, and Fogal.

Falke

Tel: +49 (0)297 27 991, www.falke.com

Falke, which dates back to 1895, is as known for its performance and technology elements as its sophisticated design. The brand's hosiery is defined by its combination of comfort and fashion and offers a pressure-free fit, run-guard construction, and body-molding properties. Highlights include Italian lace trims and elegant striped patterns.

Fogal

Rennweg 10, 8001 Zurich

Tel: +41 (0)4 42 11 79 28, www.fogal.com

Established in 1923, Fogal has long been on the front lines of hosiery innovation, bringing the first nylon stockings to Europe in 1938, as well as introducing elastic tights in the 1960s. Today the brand upholds its tradition for quality and style with more than seventy different colors and couture patterns, such as lace, animal prints, multihued stripes, and geometric patterns.

Maria La Rosa

Tel: +39 (0)2 70 12 78 55, www.marialarosa.it

EXPERT Essential Although Maria La Rosa doesn't make hosiery per se—her collection consists of socks, thigh-highs, and other accessories—the couture-like precision she employs in creating her line makes her designs a must-have in any lingerie drawer. All the textiles used in La Rosa's products are made manually on antique looms. She strictly uses natural fibers, such as cotton, linen, silk, chenille, and cashmere, and all quantities are limited. Her legwear offerings include leggings, knee socks, and over-the-knee socks in both classic and whimsical patterns, such as Fair Isle, argyle, checkerboard, polka dots, and trompe l'oeil ballet slippers.

Philippe Matignon

Tel: +39 (0)376 94 12 11,
www.philippematignon.it

The "stylist of tights," Philippe Matignon is known for his high-fashion hosiery that marries refinement and elegance with research and technology. With an active, style-conscious woman in mind, the brand offers a wide range of sophisticated designs, such as elegant pinstripes, discreet polka dots, and delicate lace. The classics collection offers a wide range of silhouettes and deniers in a multitude of basic shades.

In the details

The weight measurement
that determines the
quality of hosiery

» Measure of excellence

The term *denier* is derived from the French word for
a now obsolete small coin of little value. Denier is a
weight measurement for the knitting yarn used to
make hosiery. The base weight for hosiery of any
kind (nylon, silk, or rayon) is obtained by weighing
450 meters (1476 feet) of thread. That measurement
becomes the standard from which to determine the
caliber of the stocking. The lighter the thread, the
finer the weave and the less denier.

Thick opaque tights usually measure 70 to 100
denier and are ideal for overall coverage and
warmth. Opaque tights measure 41 to 69, semi-
opaque are 21 to 40, and sheer range from 10 to 20.
These three categories are commonly regarded as
the most ubiquitous stockings as they can serve a
variety of purposes and occasions. Anything
measuring less than 10 denier qualifies as ultra sheer
and is ideal for achieving a bare leg look.

Wolford

Kärntner Strasse 22, Vienna 1010, Austria

www.wolford.com

Founded in 1949, Wolford is a luxury leg and body-wear brand that includes hosiery, bodysuits, swimwear, and underwear. Its hosiery is distinguished by intricate patterns, exclusive weaves, and bold fashion prints, and its reputation for excellence has been furthered by high-profile collaborations with Karl Lagerfeld, Vivienne Westwood, and Emilio Pucci.

120

» Possess

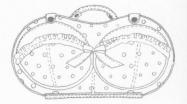

Lingerie online

Although nothing compares to shopping in the flesh, sometimes it's hard to find your favorite brand of lingerie in your city. That's when the online store comes to the rescue. Shopping the brands you know is easy, since you're already familiar with their sizing. But if you're opting for something new, buy items in your usual size, as well as one size up and one down so you have a better chance of getting the perfect fit. Always check return policies to make sure you won't get stuck with merchandise you don't want.

» **www.coco-de-mer.com**
Brands Coco de Mer, Lascivious, La Perla, Bordelle, Fleur of England, Ophelia Fancy, Princesse Tam Tam, Nichole de Carle, Stella McCartney, Damaris, and more.
Extras Art, books, jewelry, and erotic accessories.

› **www.fairefroufrou.com**
Brands Simone Pérèle, Ari Dein, The Lake & Stars, John Galliano, Kenzo, Guia la Bruna, and more.
Extras If you're in Los Angeles, you can book an appointment with a personal shopper at the Faire Frou Frou boutique. Online shoppers can narrow down their selections by choosing to shop by price, color, designer, size, or category.

» **www.nancymeyer.com**
Brands La Perla, Eres, Damaris, Nina Ricci, Kiki de Montparnasse, Jean Yu, and more.
Extras The NM Style Guide offers tips for gentlemen

Words from the wise

Jennifer Zuccarini Founder and creative director, Fleur du Mal, New York, NY

» Venturing out for vintage

With vintage lingerie you know that you have a truly unique and special piece that is also a part of history. In this sense, it is for the true lingerie lover.

Vintage lingerie tends to boast techniques that are rarely used today but which were common in the early half of the twentieth century, such as intricate hand embroidery and hand-appliquéd lace. The best place to start shopping is online. Otherwise, check vintage clothing shops—the more exclusive and designer-oriented the better—as they usually tend to have a small but well-curated selection of lingerie.

Just bear in mind when you find that perfect vintage piece, it will likely be more of a collector's item than something you'll wear every day. Even pieces made as recently as the 1960s will be very delicate and probably won't stand up to general wear-and-tear or too much laundering, let alone something that dates back to the 1920s!

looking to buy lingerie as a gift by breaking down options to "little luxuries" (stockings, candles, fragrances), "sexy lingerie," and "romantic lingerie."

» **www.glamorousamorous.com**

Brands Ell & Cee, Fifi Chachnil, Gilda & Pearl, Roberto Cavalli, Mimi Holliday, and more.

Extras The virtual fitting room gives detailed advice and tips on finding the right bra for your size and shape, as well as an extensive lingerie glossary.

» **www.miodestino.com**

Brands Aubade, Lise Charmel, Cotton Club, I.D. Sarrieri, and more.

Extras Irreverent and cheeky, this site aims to "demystify" lingerie, sleep, and swimwear for customers, and groups categories with names such as "Out of the doghouse" and "Lingerie for golfers." They also group European brands by country of origin.

» **www.cazar.de**

Brands Christies, Aubade, Roberto Cavalli, Cotton Club, Lise Charmel, Hanro, and more.

Extras Gift items include delicate handmade lingerie drawer sachets and ceramic heart-shaped objets d'art.

» **www.dessus-dessous.fr**

Brands Lise Charmel, Marie Jo, PrimaDonna, Conturelle, Aubade, Simone Pérèle, Chantelle, Passionata, and more.

Extras The site offers a wide variety of plus-size bras and swimwear and frequently puts merchandise on sale starting at 30 percent off.

Washing luxury delicates

Laundering luxury garments of any kind is a tricky endeavor, especially delicate lacy lingerie. The utmost care should be paid to washing your intimates to maintain the integrity of the material as well as the construction.

Hand washing

Handwashing is recommended for all luxury lingerie, particularly bras, and especially if it is made of lace, silk, tulle, satin, or any other delicate fabric. Soak lingerie for up to fifteen minutes in cool to lukewarm water using a delicate detergent or mild shampoo (preferably a baby shampoo). By leaving items to soak, dirt, oils, and stains will usually dissipate on their own; for tough stains, spot treat areas with some detergent or mild soap. Gently squeeze suds through the fabric or swirl the items in the soapy water.

Do not rinse your lingerie under running water as it can stretch out the fabric; instead, run clean water through the basin until all the detergent is rinsed out. Then take each item individually, fold it, and press it against the side of the basin to get out excess water—never wring out your bras or briefs! Roll them up in a clean towel to absorb as much water as possible and hang to dry.

Caring for silk

Because of the delicate characteristics of silk, never try to spot treat silk items as you will end up with a watermark that will not come out. Although silk is best ironed while still slightly wet, sleepwear and loungewear require precise ironing, thus, it is best to send these items to the dry cleaner.

Lingerie wash bags

If you absolutely must put your lingerie in the washer, place items in a mesh wash bag (preferably one that has a tight weave to reduce the risk of garments snagging or poking out). Make sure to link all bra hooks ahead of time to reduce stretching and run the machine on a gentle cycle. Never put bras in the dryer as the heat can break down and melt materials. Cotton undergarments are generally safe for machine wash, although they should always be run through a gentle cycle.

Delicate detergents

Although it may sound suspicious, specially formulated detergent for your delicates is not just a marketing gimmick. Most of these washes are less chemically treated than regular detergent and are lighter on fragrance, thus putting less stress on fine fabrics.

The Laundress Delicate Wash

www.thelaundress.com

Non-toxic, biodegradable, and allergen-free, The Laundress Delicate Wash can be used for both hand and machine washing and is formulated to remove perspiration, body oils, and stains.

Tocca Laundry Delicate Fine Fabric Wash

www.tocca.com

This gentle soap is suitable for hand and machine washing and comes in four delicate fragrances—grapefruit cucumber, rose, blood orange, and pomegranate.

Forever New Fabric Care Wash

www.forevernew.com

Widely regarded as one of the best products on the market, Forever New is organic and biodegradable and is formulated to extend the life of delicate garments. Its natural base of sodas and citrus leaves no residue and preserves elasticity.

Compagnie de Provence Liquid Detergent for Delicate Textiles and Lingerie With Marseille Soap

www.compagniedeprovence.com

This detergent is non-scented and enriched with Marseille soap and silk extracts. It is composed from vegetable-based active agents and is phosphate-free and biodegradable. One 25.4-ounce bottle is good for twenty-five hand washes.

Soyelle Lingerie Wash

www.soyelle.com

Packaged in single doses, Soyelle Lingerie Wash is ideal for travel as it removes dirt, oil, and perspiration from lingerie, as well as chlorine, lotion, and salt water from swimwear. Drop one pouch into one gallon of cool water (it dissolves the plastic casing as well) and soak lingerie. The detergent is phosphate-free, biodegradable, and prevents the yellowing of fabric.

UNIQUE » RARE » LITTLE-KNOWN » **ULTIMATE EXPERT**

Saramae slips In the 1940s to 1960s, there was one lingerie brand that stood apart from the rest: Saramae Lingerie. Sold at high-end department stores, such as Saks Fifth Avenue, Saramae, whose offices were located on Madison Avenue in New York, distinguished itself by creating half slips that were often more beautiful than the skirts covering them. Made from chiffon and silk-nylon blends, the slips featured layers of imported lace and exquisite embroideries and designs, and could easily pass as couture skirts by today's standards. It is difficult to find Saramae items today, because most vintage collectors are reluctant to let go of any they might have, but eBay has been known to carry a few pieces from time to time.

Travel and storage

All the meticulous folding and strategic packing in the world can't make up for the beating luggage takes when it travels from the car trunk to the cargo compartment. By putting your lingerie in a dedicated lingerie bag, you can minimize the chance of bras and briefs getting tangled up with other items in your suitcase. A good idea is to buy three or four lingerie bags: one for bras, one for briefs, one for hosiery, and one to store all your dirty laundry throughout your trip.

The Bra Bag

The ideal way to store bras during travel, however, is to put them in a protective case that will prevent them from twisting or getting snagged on anything else. The Brag Company's revolutionary Bra Bag (www.thebragcompany.com) stores bras in a zippered hard case that holds one to six bras and can accommodate up to a size 36C or 32D. The company also makes the Buxom Bra Bag for bras up to size 36G or 38F, and a Panty Pak that has zippered

» The Bra Bag, which holds up to six bras

compartments for your clean and used briefs. Similarly, the Braza Bra Travel Bag (www.brazabra.com) also stores bras in a moulded case and fits up to three A to C cup bras, while the larger size fits up to three E cups. The travel bag also has two mesh pockets for jewelry or other small items.

Drawer storage

Once home, lay your bras flat in a drawer and stack them one on top of the other to save space. Or place them on a mold to maintain their shape, but don't put more than three bras on one mold or they risk misshaping or flattening the cups.

From underwear to lingerie

Frederick Mellinger, founder of world-renowned lingerie brand Frederick's of Hollywood, returned to the United States after serving in World War II, bringing back with him an understanding of and reverence for European lingerie.

Mellinger left his first mark by dressing Hollywood stars in black lingerie, rather than the standard white. Then in the early 1950s, he invented the first push-up bra, dubbed "The Rising Star." Today Frederick's offers fifteen different styles of push-up bras and has furthered the technology with the Liquid Lift collection of rosewater-and-oil-infused padded bras that naturally mold to the shape of the breast.

Alterations and repairs

A changing silhouette or wear-and-tear of your favorite bra doesn't have to mean investing in a new lingerie wardrobe. There are professionals who can alter undergarments for you. Although most department stores will offer to do alterations or repairs using their own in-house seamstresses or tailors, they probably won't be specialists at altering lingerie. If your local dry cleaner is trustworthy enough to launder your delicates, they will likely have a reputable person on hand to do alterations, too. Otherwise, check in with your favorite speciality lingerie shop. If they don't have someone in-house, they will likely be able to suggest a reputable tailor or specialist seamstress to you.

Dor-ne Corset Shoppe

8126 Georgia Ave, Silver Spring, MD 20910

Tel: (301) 589 5151, www.dornecorset.com

Known throughout the Washington, DC, area as specialists in hard-to-fit sizes, Dor-ne Corset Shoppe carries an array of lingerie from brands such as Panache and Goddess, ranging from 30A to 52J. Each customer who walks in the store is tended to by her own fitter, and the in-store seamstresses are qualified to tailor any garment for any occasion. They will also alter items not purchased in-store.

Rigby & Peller

(for details see page 40)

The customized experience at Rigby & Peller doesn't end at the cash register. If you require alterations done on any item purchased in-store, a qualified fitter will advise you on alterations, pin your garment, and send it to one of the specialized seamstresses in the workroom. Common alterations include taking in or letting out bra bands, adding darts to the side of a bra, sewing pads into bra cups for extra lift, and adding mastectomy pockets to bras and swimwear.

Town Shop

2273 Broadway, New York, NY 10024

Tel: (212) 787 2762, www.townshop.com

Since 1888, Town Shop has been specializing in fitting customers ranging from size AA to JJ, garnering a reputation as one of New York's most famous lingerie boutiques. Today the store carries renowned brands, such as Cosabella, Wolford, and Chantelle, and offers free on-site alterations.

>> Discover

Museums and exhibits

For a more in-depth look at lingerie and textiles through the ages and how they translate to today, check out these artistic venues.

The Metropolitan Museum of Art Costume Institute

1000 Fifth Ave, New York, NY 10028

Tel: (212) 535 7710, www.metmuseum.org

The MET comprises more than two million pieces of art from around the world and boasts an extensive selection of historical and modern fashion in its highly acclaimed Costume Institute. Perhaps best known for its annual gala that attracts a who's who of the art and fashion worlds, the Costume Institute has a wide selection of vintage and modern lingerie from designers such as Paul Smith, Dolce & Gabbana, and Calvin Klein, although it isn't always on display. Contact the museum ahead of time to learn about current fashion exhibits.

V&A South Kensington

Cromwell Road, London, SW7 2RL

Tel: +44 (0)207 942 2000, www.vam.ac.uk

The Textiles and Fashion collection at the Victoria & Albert Museum includes a vast range of corsets, bras, hoops, stays, and bodysuits dating as far back as the eighteenth century, and includes items from Rigby & Peller, Dior, Calvin Klein, and Agent Provocateur.

Fashion Museum

Assembly Rooms, Bennett Street, Bath, BA1 2QH

Tel: +44 (0)122 547 7789,
www.museumofcostume.co.uk

Focusing on contemporary and historical dress, this museum has an inclusive collection of womenswear, menswear, accessories, and knitwear dating back to the eighteenth century. Among the collection is a small sampling of corsets from the eighteenth and nineteenth centuries.

Musée du Costume et de la Dentelle

rue de la Violette, 12 B-1000 Brussels

Tel: +32 (0)22 13 44 50,
www.brussels.be/artdet.cfm?id=4209&

Established in 1977, the Costume and Lace Museum is dedicated to highlighting Brussels's local textile industry from the eighteenth to the mid-twentieth centuries. The focus is on lace and embroidery techniques, and past exhibits have included the technicolor fabrics of the 1960s as well as embroidery from the Art Nouveau period.

Musée de la Mode et du Textile

107 rue de Rivoli, 75001 Paris

Tel: +33 (0)144 55 57 50, www.lesartsdecoratifs.fr

Located in the Louvre, the Musée de la Mode et du Textile features printed cottons, laces, tapestries, and embroideries that date back to the seventh century and is part of the larger Arts Décoratifs collection. In 1981, the latter joined with the Union Française des Arts du Costume and today boasts more than eighty-one thousand works, including pieces from Dior, Vionnet, and Poiret.

Galleria del Costume

Piazza Pitti 1, Florence 50125

Tel: +39 (0)5 52 38 87 13,
www.uffizi.firenze.it/musei/costume

Located in the historic Pitti Palace overlooking Florence's majestic Boboli Gardens, the Galleria del Costume comprises six thousand items from the sixteenth to the twentieth centuries, including costumes and accessories.

The Audie Murphy American Cotton Museum

600 Interstate 30, East Greenville, TX 75403

Tel: (903) 450 4502, www.cottonmuseum.com

Home to the Henson-Kickernick Lingerie Collection that features many of the company's lingerie prototypes as well as antique pieces, the American Cotton Museum is dedicated to the history of the American cotton industry.

Bella Blush

Tel: (703) 823 3155, www.bella-blush.com

Not quite a traditional gallery exhibit, Bella Blush incorporates art into the shopping experience by choosing to unveil new collections every season at a different contemporary art gallery in Washington, DC. Glamor and style come together at the Salon Show Date events, which feature Bella Blush's range of luxury lingerie from brands such as Lascivious,

Gilda & Pearl, Mimi Holliday, Marie Jo, and more, and run a limited period of time. Attendees receive special offers, buyer benefits, and discounts.

German Historical Museum

Zeughaus und Ausstellungshalle von I. M. Pei,
Unter den Linden 2, 10117 Berlin

Tel: +49 (0)30 2030 4444, www.dhm.de

With emphasis placed on historical events, the German Historical Museum's Clothing and Textiles collection includes a ribbon dating back to the Seven Year War of 1756, pantaloons from the French Revolution, as well as corsets and underwear from the eighteenth and nineteenth centuries.

137

Further reading and resources

The Lingerie Post

www.thelingeriepost.com

An informative blog on all things lingerie, with a special focus on luxury and the world's most famous designers and brands. The site includes reviews of the latest collections, profiles of new designers and collections, firsthand photos from catwalk shows, listings of online sales, and Lingerie TV, a compilation of new and exciting commercials and streamed fashion shows.

Petite Coquette

www.petite-coquette.co.uk

Luxury is at the core of this website that features the latest collections from the most exclusive brands, such as La Perla, Ell & Cee, and Agent Provocateur. Special features include a size guide, information on lingerie sales, a shopping guide, and tidbits about lingerie in the entertainment world.

Upper Cup

www.blog.uppercup.com

A dedicated blog for the Upper Cup e-commerce site that sells lingerie ranging exclusively from D through to L cups, this site leaves all talk of brands and sizing to its mother site and focuses on news pertaining to the world of plus-size lingerie, including swimwear, maternity, and shapewear collections. Posts include firsthand accounts from plus-size models, special offers, tips on shopping for plus-size lingerie, and contests.

Lingerie Talk

www.lingerietalk.com

A relative newcomer to the online lingerie news scene, Lingerie Talk is an independent Canadian website that focuses on new collections and launches, as well as tidbits of news from around the world that pertain to lingerie and its many facets. The site also includes special deals and sales exclusive to their readers.

Lingerie Blog

www.lingerieblog.co.uk

A one-stop blog for lingerie news, trends, offers, and shopping, Lingerie Blog also offers retailers and brands online courses in optimizing their websites for marketing and e-commerce purposes.

Frou Frou Fashionista

www.froufroufashionista.blogspot.com

Frou Frou Fashionista is a luxury lingerie blog that focuses on the finest intimate apparel from around the world, as well as from Faire Frou Frou, a boutique lingerie store based in California, which offers lingerie from various top designers and brands, including Strumpet & Pink, Ari Dein, and Fleur of England.

I Love My Bra

www.Ilovemybra.com

> A lingerie blog offering advice on luxury brands and designers, including links and lingerie reviews, the latest industry news and trends, information on care and bra styles.

The Lingerie Addict

www.thelingerieaddict.com

> The Lingerie Addict started in 2008 as a small blog about stockings, founded by Cora Harrington, a.k.a. Treacle Tart, a twenty-something Seattle resident. The Lingerie Addict is devoted to covering both high-end and low-end lingerie brands, independent and mass-market companies.

Liaison Dangereuse

www.liaison-dangereuse.com/lingerie-blog/

> Liaison Dangereuse is an online luxury lingerie boutique, with a blog called Lingerie Styles. Written (in German) by a fashion writer who has worked in Milan and Paris, the blog keeps readers updated on the latest industry news and collections.

Glossary

Acetate A synthetic fiber with a silky appearance.

Bias cut The forty-five-degree direction in which a piece of woven fabric is cut to accentuate the body's lines and drape softly.

Camisole A short, sleeveless garment often with thin straps.

Cantilever A type of construction that allows for overhang without external support.

Charmeuse A fine, semi-lustrous crepe.

Chemise A loose, one-piece undergarment.

Control top Often used in hosiery, it is a shaping panel that flattens the abdomen and smoothes the hips.

Coutil A woven cloth used specifically in corset making; it has a high cotton content, resists stretching, and inhibits penetration of the corset's bones.

Crêpe de Chine A silk, wool or polyester fabric of gauzy texture with a crisp appearance.

Darts A seam where fabric has been taken in to mold to the body's curves; can be part of

the original design or a result of alterations.

Duchess satin A heavy, shiny fabric often used in bridal couture.

Dupioni A thick, irregular satin.

Eyelet An embroidery that uses small perforations.

Featherbone A lightweight bone for corsetry made from the quills of domestic fowl.

Georgette A sheer crepe with a pebbly surface.

Grosgrain A strong corded fabric.

Guipure A heavy, large-patterned decorative lace.

Jacquard A fabric with an intricate weave or pattern.

Jersey A plain fabric made of wool, cotton, nylon, rayon, or silk.

Laser cut A technique of cutting fabrics with precise lasers to minimize fraying and eliminate seams.

Macramé A lace or fringe made by knotting threads in a geometric pattern.

Mastectomy pocket A special pocket sewn into the cup(s) of a bra where a silicone breast form can be secured in place.

Mercerized cotton A treatment for cotton fabric and thread that gives fabric a lustrous appearance.

Microfiber A fine, soft polyester fabric.

Mille fleur An all-over pattern of small flowers.

Modal A type of rayon made from the cellulose of beech trees; it is more water resistant than cotton and doesn't shrink or fade.

Mohair A yarn made from the long silky hair of the Angora goat.

Molded Pre-formed thick foam cups in bras.

Pinking shears Scissors whose blades are saw-toothed and cut a zigzag pattern; used predominantly in cutting seams in vintage lingerie.

Piqué A durable cotton.

PVC A type of vinyl.

Seamless Having no seams, thus eliminating the possibility of a visible panty line.

Shapewear A foundation garment that smoothes and streamlines the figure.

Silk habotai A fabric similar to chiffon but opaque, with a glossy, lustrous finish.

Supima A high-quality cotton.

Tulle A sheer silk, rayon, or nylon net.

Whalebone Also known as baleen, the filtering structure in the mouth of most whales; it is composed of keratin protein and was used for making items that require flexibility and strength.

Index

143

144